SAGE was founded in 1965 by Sara Miller McCune to support the dissemination of usable knowledge by publishing innovative and high-quality research and teaching content. Today, we publish over 900 journals, including those of more than 400 learned societies, more than 800 new books per year, and a growing range of library products including archives, data, case studies, reports, and video. SAGE remains majority-owned by our founder, and after Sara's lifetime will become owned by a charitable trust that secures our continued independence.

Los Angeles | London | New Delhi | Singapore | Washington DC | Melbourne

Advance Praise

'Lynching is an act of terror. It is a weapon of a psychological war waged against people, Muslims in particular, but also Dalits. It is to tell their youth that they are not safe and that the killers can pick anyone they wish to, anywhere, anytime. Lynching is not limited by geography and cannot be contained as a communal riot can be by bringing in the army. Ziya Us Salam's timely study exposes the threat and the politics. For me, it is clear: If Muslims are not safe, no minority is safe, even if their youth are not being lynched.'

John Dayal
Senior journalist, author and human rights activist

'*Lynch Files* makes for compulsory reading for anyone who wants to understand how the largest democracy in the world was coerced into maintaining stoic silence over the broad daylight lynching of its own citizens just because they belonged to a particular faith or caste configuration. Ziya Us Salam succeeds in dissecting the ideological undercurrents behind these ghastly hate crimes and exposes their diabolical modus operandi. The author's analysis about 'lynching' being the new substitute for 'communal riots' is veracious as these 'low-profile' but 'high-intensity' incidents have achieved their sinister purpose of creating communal antagonism. A must-read for all concerned citizens of this nation.'

Muhammad Salim Engineer
Secretary-General, Jamaat-e-Islami Hind

'With Upanishadic prayers and Rumi's poetry, and Ramakrishna's ecstasy and Gandhi's contemplative practice, as I look at Ziya Us Salam's revealing text in Lynch Files, it makes me feel ashamed of the ugliness of a de-spiritualized majoritarian doctrine. From Alwar to Chittorgarh, and from Hapur to Jammu, an insightful documentation and analysis of 'Lynch Files' is bound to make a sensitive reader feel the meaning of being born as Akhlaq or Mohsin Shaikh in a non-secular/non-spiritual culture that allows the nasty politics of *gau rakshaks* to insult the foundations of a civilization nurtured by the likes of Kabir and Tagore. A must-read!'

Avijit Pathak
Professor of Sociology, Jawaharlal Nehru University, New Delhi

'Lynching is a word added to the national lexicon in the four years of the rule of the Bharatiya Janata Party. Reports of people being lynched by mobs have become routine and no longer excite the moral imagination of India. The target of these lynchings have been primarily Muslims. What is special about the murders of Muslims by the mobs is that they cannot even protest as Muslims. While there have been cases of Dalits being killed by mobs and also some stray incidents of other kinds of lynching, there is no denying the fact that killing of Muslims in this manner has a genocidal tone to it.'

'Ziya Us Salam performs a painful duty of recording this episode in the history of independent secular India for us and for the posterity. The book very convincingly demonstrates that rather than being isolated and unconnected unfortunate incidents, these lynchings are an integral part of the genocidal project of the Bharatiya Janata Party directed mainly against the Muslims.'

Apoorvanand
Professor, Department of Hindi, Faculty of Arts, University of Delhi

LYNCH FILES

LYNCH FILES

The Forgotten Saga of Victims of Hate Crime

ZIYA US SALAM

Los Angeles | London | New Delhi
Singapore | Washington DC | Melbourne

Copyright © Ziya Us Salam, 2019

All rights reserved. No part of this book may be reproduced or utilized in any form or by any means, electronic or mechanical, including photocopying, recording, or by any information storage or retrieval system, without permission in writing from the publisher.

First published in 2019 by

SAGE Publications India Pvt Ltd
B1/I-1 Mohan Cooperative Industrial Area
Mathura Road, New Delhi 110 044, India
www.sagepub.in

SAGE Publications Inc
2455 Teller Road
Thousand Oaks, California 91320, USA

SAGE Publications Ltd
1 Oliver's Yard, 55 City Road
London EC1Y 1SP, United Kingdom

SAGE Publications Asia-Pacific Pte Ltd
18 Cross Street #10-10/11/12
China Square Central
Singapore 048423

Published by Vivek Mehra for SAGE Publications India Pvt Ltd, typeset in 10.5/15 pts Avenir LT Std by Fidus Design Pvt. Ltd., Chandigarh.

Library of Congress Cataloging-in-Publication Data
Name: Ziya Us Salam, author.
Title: Lynch files: the forgotten saga of victims of hate crime/Ziya Us Salam.
Description: New Delhi, India: SAGE Publications India, 2019.
Identifiers: LCCN 2018055334 | ISBN 9789353282196 (pbk.: alk. paper) | ISBN 9789353282202 (epub 2.0) | ISBN 9789353282219 (ebook)
Subjects: LCSH: Lynching—India—History. | Hate crimes—India—History.
Classification: LCC HV6471.I4 Z59 2019 | DDC 364.1/34—dc23
LC record available at https://lccn.loc.gov/2018055334

ISBN: 978-93-532-8219-6 (PB)

SAGE Team: Namarita Kathait, Guneet Kaur, Kumar Indra Mishra and Rajinder Kaur

[
To my lovely sisters,
Baji and Bajiya,
(known to the world as
Sayyeda Muslima and
Sayyeda Sajida)
for being there for me
through thick and thin.
]

Thank you for choosing a SAGE product!
If you have any comment, observation or feedback,
I would like to personally hear from you.

Please write to me at **contactceo@sagepub.in**

Vivek Mehra, Managing Director and CEO, SAGE India.

Bulk Sales

SAGE India offers special discounts
for purchase of books in bulk.
We also make available special imprints
and excerpts from our books on demand.

For orders and enquiries, write to us at

Marketing Department
SAGE Publications India Pvt Ltd
B1/I-1, Mohan Cooperative Industrial Area
Mathura Road, Post Bag 7
New Delhi 110044, India

E-mail us at **marketing@sagepub.in**

Subscribe to our mailing list
Write to **marketing@sagepub.in**

This book is also available as an e-book.

Contents

Foreword by Jignesh Mevani — ix
Preface — xiii
Acknowledgements — xxv

FILE 1. LYNCHING

A Substitute for Communal Riots 3
Cow, a Sacred or a Political Animal?.................9
The Oft-present Political Hand........................14
Common Maximum Programme: Similarities in Lynching Incidents 21
Gaurakshini Sabhas: Walk Down to the Nineteenth Century..28
Bhartiya Gau Raksha Dal: Part-time Professionals........33
Mind of a *Gau Rakshak*: All Hate, No Love? 41

FILE 2. MUSLIMS: EASY TARGETS?

Omen of Things to Come 49
Dadri: Akhlaq 49
Pune: Mohsin Shaikh 59
The *Gau Rakshaks* of Rajasthan 64
Alwar Lynchings..64
Chittorgarh Lynchings 82
Rajsamand: Afrazul..86
Horrifying Mutilations in Haryana.......................92

Ballabhgarh: Junaid on Delhi–Mathura Train 92
Kurukshetra: Mustain Abbas 100
Lynched and Filmed in Uttar Pradesh **102**
Hapur: Qasim and Samiuddin 102
Hanged by the Mob in Jharkhand **113**
Ramgarh: Alimuddin Ansari 113
Giridih: Usman Ansari 120
Latehar: Mazloom Ansari and Imtiaz 125
Killings in the Name of the Cow **132**
Jammu: Sammi 132
Himachal Pradesh: Noman 134
Normalizing Lynching **139**
Satna: Siraj Khan and Shakeel 139
Delhi: Rizwan, Kamil and Ashfaq 144

FILE 3. THE MOB NOW TARGETS DALITS

At the Mercy of Upper Castes 151
Hamirpur: Chimma 151
Una: The Lynchings and the Dalit Uprising 154

FILE 4. LYNCHED AND FORGOTTEN!

When Tragedies Were Dismissed **163**
10 States and Many More Lynchings 163

FILE 5. AFTERMATH

Supreme Court Shows the Way 179
Desecrating Hate, Bigotry and Everything that Leads to Lynching **186**

About the Author   **194**

Foreword

In his first Independence Day address at the historic Red Fort in 2014, Prime Minister Narendra Modi called for a 10-year moratorium on communal and caste violence. The minorities and the Dalits heaved a sigh of relief. Their worst fears seemed dispelled. It seemed Mr Modi had turned a new leaf as the prime minister. Some were even beginning to believe his government's slogan of *Sabka Saath, Sabka Vikas* (Collective Efforts, Inclusive Growth). Too soon, as it turned out. All the talk of abjuring caste and communal violence proved just that. In less than a week of the new government being sworn in, a Muslim techie was lynched to death in Pune as he stopped over to pick his dinner after evening prayers. The incident should have shaken the conscience of the nation. But in June 2014, the nation was high on the opium of promised development. It needed the brutal and unpardonable lynching of Muhammed Akhlaq to apprise us with the reality of our times. Here was a case of a man sleeping in his bedroom being dragged out and done to death by cow militia, falsely called *gau rakshaks* by the media. Rather than offering words of solace to the bereaved family, the prime minister kept quiet. In his silence was a tacit approval of the gory deed. His minister Mahesh Sharma went a step further by wrapping our national flag around the body of one of the men accused of killing Akhlaq. Suddenly, it seemed a patriotic thing to kill a Muslim in his sleep and dress up the murder as one of a cow killer. Akhlaq was not around to speak for himself. His family's cries fell on deaf ears.

Just as the Muslim community was grappling with the reality of lynching, their fellow downtrodden Dalit community woke up to the news of a 90-year-old Dalit man being attacked, then being doused with kerosene before being set on fire in Hamirpur in Uttar Pradesh. His crime? He had dared to go to a temple monopolized by upper castes. Even as he was burnt to death, no bystander came forward to help. This was the New India in all its casteist and communal hues that nobody had bargained for.

Yet the prime minister maintained silence. On Twitter, he greeted sportsmen and fellow politicians on their birthdays. He had no words for Akhlaq or Chimma. Lynching was an ugly aberration. It did not stay that way for long. After Akhlaq, the Muslim community faced a regular spectre of attacks, humiliation and death on the roads, simply because some Hindutva brigade members believed they had killed a cow, or consumed beef. What was in an individual's fridge became the responsibility of the state. With Usman, Alimuddin and Pehlu Khan's lynching, it became the new normal.

However, there was another parallel strand to this murder of the innocent. Probably feeling emboldened by the absence of state condemnation in the instances of lynching of Muslim men by largely upper caste cow militia, they decided to train their guns at the penury-ridden Dalit community. We had the macabre spectacle of four Dalit youths, stripped to their waist and tied to a jeep, being thrashed by upper caste men in Una. Once again, the masses watched in tacit acceptance. Pray,

Lynch Files

what was the crime of these four Dalit boys? Skinning a dead cow! Their pleas that the animal was already dead when they started skinning, and they had not killed it, fell on deaf ears. In New India, the dominant religion, the dominant caste was beginning to decide who will eat what and who will follow which profession. The society at large once again swung into action only when Dalits refused to clear cow carcasses. As one of their leaders said, 'If the cow is regarded as a mother by upper castes when alive, she cannot be Dalits' responsibility when dead'.

This constant attack on the dignity of the Dalits and Muslims underlines a feeling that society overrides the state. The Constitution abolished untouchability. It does not allow discrimination based on religion, caste or gender, either. The law might protect the victims, but the society in such cases rides roughshod over it. The state, in all such cases, does not harass the minorities or Dalits. Rather, it is left to non-state actors. These non-state actors are the ones who have no regard for the law of the land, and under the garb of their faith, attack the innocent. The state stays quiet.

In *Lynch Files*, seasoned journalist and author Ziya Us Salam analyses the link between lynch mobs and organs of the state. 'He gives us a lowdown to most lynch victims and tells us how the state has often been seen with the perpetrators of violence'. The book covers a whole range of assaults on the minorities and the Dalits, from Gujarat to Assam, from Jammu and Kashmir to Karnataka. Done with characteristic research and sincerity, Salam's *Lynch Files* is a timely window to New India. It deserves a careful reading and a place on your bookshelf for years to come.

Jignesh Mevani

Foreword

Preface

In the summer of 2017, Eid-ul-Fitr came with a grim reminder of 1975. It was the first time since the Emergency that the Muslim community had decided to abstain from celebrating the festival that marks the culmination of 30 days of fasting in Ramzan. Back in 1975, the community had protested vehemently against Sanjay Gandhi's relocation and sterilization campaigns. Women stood guard against men chosen for sterilization at Dujana House in the old city, and hundreds of women and children sat on the road to prevent demolition of their colonies near Turkman Gate. Imam Abdullah Bukhari of Old Delhi's historic Jama Masjid had asked the men who had gathered for Eid namaz to offer their prayers, and go back home quiet and sombre without the traditional pomp and gaiety. Armbands were not so popular then; instead, some black flags were waved at the mosque. This was the community's retaliation for a series of often-done-under duress sterilization or relocation to far-flung Trilokpuri or Mangolpuri.

Year 2017 offered a different challenge. Young Junaid, not out of teenage yet, and already a hafiz (one who had memorized the Quran) was lynched aboard a Delhi–Mathura train in the presence of his elder brother and friends. The attackers, actually fellow passengers, threw him out of the train. He was dubbed a beefeater, hence deserving of death. None of the fellow passengers came to his rescue. This in a country where until not long ago, it was not unusual for non-Muslim passengers to make room for a Muslim passenger to offer his namaz sitting on the seat, or even a group to offer a quick prayer in congregation. In fact, our trains were a miniature replica of persistent foreign invasions in our history. With each invader, there was initial resistance, then grudging accommodation, before there came about a more cordial exchange. It was the same from the Aryans to the Mughals via the Delhi Sultans. On our trains too, in the years gone by, there would be general melee for a seat as soon as the train arrived at the railway station. In the unreserved section, people would rush to get to a seat. Grabbing one was an achievement it itself. It left the aged, and the less agile, pacing up and down in search of an elusive seat. However, as the train moved, some families would 'adjust' a little bit to accommodate a woman or an old man standing there. After some time, the occupants would start chatting, gradually warming up to each other to the extent that they would talk of exploring job opportunities, matrimonial alliances, etc. Of course, they would offer food to each other, exchange phone numbers and then alight at their respective stations. In between, they would usually move their trunks or a shoulder bag further below the seat, and huddle up on one seat so that the bearded maulana next to them could offer his Maghrib (sunset) prayer on the other seat. No one ever objected. It was common courtesy. For a few minutes that the maulana said his prayers, all the chitchat would stop. Everybody would make sure that the prayer would not be disturbed.

In 2017, that was a fading memory, as the passengers on the Delhi–Mathura train stood as mute witness while Junaid was subjected to worst communal abuses, hit repeatedly by

Lynch Files

a group of young men, taunted for his alleged food habits, before finally being killed, thrown off at a platform. Just as nobody on the train uttered a word for the defenceless Junaid, the prime minister of India remained unmoved, his selective silence a stain upon speech. His party leaders objected to raising a voice for Junaid with their whataboutery of Kashmiri Pandits, etc. Upset, dejected and hurt, the Muslim community expressed its anguish by wearing black armbands to Eid prayers. The celebrations were muted, the faces grim. In fact, many mosques in Delhi, Agra and Jaipur reported lower than usual attendance for Eid prayers. The shopkeepers, likewise, reported a lull in sales on *Chand ki raat* (eve of Eid), when Muslim women usually step out in groups for last-minute shopping which often culminates with the application of henna on young girls' hands. Fear and anger had gripped the community. A community already feeling hemmed in retreated further into its shell.

Like in 1975, the community looked for a ray of hope. It was not forthcoming. Back then, Indira Gandhi was inaccessible and arrogant. Now, Narendra Modi was distant and aloof.

Junaid's was not the only instance when a helpless Muslim man had been cornered by a murderous mob, and had death delivered to him without prior warning, in the most brutal of ways. There was Pehlu Khan, a dairy farmer, who was hit for full 90 minutes in Alwar by the so-called *gau rakshaks*, actually murderers under the cloak of cow protectors. The middle-aged man could not take constant torture and humiliation. He succumbed to his injuries soon after, but not before he had named his attackers. As the nation in general, and the Muslim community in particular, waited along with Pehlu's family for arrest, and maybe, exemplary punishment for the attackers, an air of dismay soon followed. All the men accused of murder

Preface

were declared innocent by the Rajasthan police despite a dying man's declaration having the value of evidence. It was New India. You could kill a Muslim man in bright daylight on a highway and hope to walk free. This travesty would have surprised only those who had forgotten the Chittorgarh stripping, and assault incident of a young Muslim man and his companions. The man was videotaped lying naked on a barren piece of land, two *gau rakshaks*' feet planted firmly on his face. Later, he was paraded naked around the town. People watched and went back to business. Attacking and humiliating Muslims was the new normal. The media remained largely oblivious. Humiliating and stripping a Muslim were deemed not newsworthy.

Then there were assaults on Muslim dairy farmers and meat merchants in states such as Jharkhand, Madhya Pradesh, Uttar Pradesh, Haryana, Rajasthan and Himachal Pradesh. In each of the states, a man was killed by cow vigilantes. The script was familiar: A man would be accused of cow slaughter, a mob would lynch him, the police will file a first information report (FIR) against the victims, even the dead, and file another one against random or unnamed attackers who would soon be given bail. In this orchestrated violence, no Muslim was safe in the rural belt; from Akhlaq dragged out of his bedroom in Dadri and done to death to Mazloom and Imtiaz kidnapped with their livestock in Jharkhand to Junaid going back home by train after Eid shopping, and on to Qasim going to purchase goats with all his savings, two days after Eid in Hapur. There was another common factor: The men would be attacked either a little before Eid or a little after it, making sure that the community approached the festival with lurking fear, foreboding and danger. Clearly, joy had been snuffed out of their lives ever since a temple in Dadri rallied people on its public announcement system, telling them a calf had been slaughtered. No evidence was ever presented, but Akhlaq paid with his life for the allegation, cruelty and brutality marking his end in September 2015.

There was nothing spontaneous about lynching. Although apparently spontaneous, all such actions were well-organized affairs, where the perpetrators knew beforehand that their public display of violence or even its recording or sharing it with a larger audience on the social media was not going to have an adverse impact on their life.

Most of the cases happened in states ruled by the Bharatiya Janata Party and its associates, pointing to political complicity in the actions. The niggling suspicion being proved right when the Union Minister Mahesh Sharma, who had only cursorily visited the family of Akhlaq following his murder, sent one of the murder accused on his last journey wrapped in the national Tricolour. Killing a Muslim was akin to fighting on the border, and deserving of equal rewards for the 'valour'! Not surprising that his colleagues in Jharkhand and Rajasthan did not acquit themselves any better. The Harvard-educated Union Minister Jayant Sinha did not deem it inappropriate to garland the men convicted of the murder of Alimuddin Ansari in Jharkhand's Ramgarh. And Rajasthan MLA Gyan Dev Ahuja, never accused of sobriety or secularism, pronounced the men accused of killing Rakbar as 'innocent', and sought their immediate release. He waited for no investigation, no court order. In the political vocabulary of our times, a lynch victim was never a victim alone. He was also the instigator, the one who provoked the mob into killing him, almost like inviting death home. Clearly, in political lexicon, a Muslim could be killed for no crime except that he was a Muslim. Amid this blatant defence of the indefensible, the number of lynching cases piled up. From Kashmir to Madhya Pradesh, from Rajasthan to Jharkhand,

men were called cow killers, and killed by *gau rakshaks*! As the political bosses ho-hummed, dilly-dallied, *IndiaSpend* took the lid off the entire exercise: Its two databases on mob violence—due to child-lifting rumours and bovine-related hate violence—recorded 80 cases where attackers outnumbered the victims, and 41 deaths by such lynchings between 2014 and March 2018. Soon, Qasim and Rakbar were added to the casualty list. These figures ran parallel to government figures. It was revealed by the Ministry of Home Affairs, 'Between 2014 and March 3, 2018, 45 persons were killed in 40 cases of mob lynching across nine states, and at least 217 persons had been arrested'. Considering a number of states such as Bihar, West Bengal, Madhya Pradesh, Chhattisgarh and Delhi had not provided the data for their states, the actual figures were likely to be much higher. *IndiaSpend* rubbed it in,

> Since 2010, 86 attacks fuelled by the suspicion of cow slaughter or beef consumption, have been reported in English media across the country. About 98 per cent of these attacks occurred post-May 2014, after the Bharatiya Janata Party (BJP) and Prime Minister Narendra Modi assumed power. At least 33 persons were killed in these attacks—29 or 88% of whom were Muslim.[1]

The constant cruelty inflicted on Muslims has not been the only occasion of the society hitting out at those on the margins. The Dalits too have been at the receiving end. It started barely a couple of weeks after Akhlaq's sad end. We had a tearful case of a 90-year-old Dalit man being denied access to a temple in Hamirpur in Uttar Pradesh. He had set out with his wife and younger brother for a *darshan* at an upper caste temple

---

[1] IndiaSpend. Available at: https://factchecker.in/minister-to-parliament-no-data-on-lynching-here-they-are-including-governments-own/

 Lynch Files

when he was stopped by a dominant caste man. Upon his refusal, he was first attacked with an axe and then set on fire. However, the incident failed to rouse us from slumber. That was accomplished when four Dalit boys were subjected to ignominy of public stripping and thrashing after being found skinning a dead cow in Una in Gujarat. Later, the members of the Bhartiya Gau Raksha Dal (BGRD) took them to a nearby town and again thrashed them with sticks and iron rods after tying them to a vehicle. They were also paraded half-naked on the road. The photograph of the four man tied to a jeep and being attacked with rods and belts went viral. It evoked the kind of sympathy that came the way of Ansari, the man who, in 2002, became the symbol of Gujarat violence with his picture of tears in his eyes, fear on his face and folded hands. The Dalit boys won a reprieve of sorts thanks to the prompt and aggressive response of the community members who took out a rally in support of the victims and refused to skin dead cows. Later, the Dalit men refused to dispose of the dead animals, with an activist Bezwada Wilson clearly arguing that if the cow, when alive, was a mother to Brahmins, she cannot be the responsibility of the Dalits when dead. Upcoming leader Jignesh Mevani instilled in the community a sense of power, a sense of belonging. The robust response to Una ensured that no more Dalit lynching incidents were reported for the next couple of years. Of course it did not mean that the society had started nursing notions of egalitarianism. There were grassroots incidents of humiliation of the community. For example, when an old man was forced to lick the saliva of an upper caste man. Or, a Dalit woman was forced to carry her slippers in her hand when passing in front of the house of an upper caste man. There was violence too when a Dalit boy, astride a horse, took out his wedding procession from the locality of upper castes. The community though was saved more lynching after Una, unlike the Muslims where

first Mohsin Shaikh and then Akhlaq opened the gateway to hate violence.

With such mayhem all around, the word 'lynch' entered the vocabulary of the common Indian. People went back to their dictionaries to search for the exact meaning of the term 'lynch' and discovered that it means, 'to kill someone for an alleged offense without a legal trial'. Incidentally, the origin of the term goes back to the mid-eighteenth- and nineteenth-century America. It became a more common way of doling out perceived justice by a mob around the mid-nineteenth Century in America. The instances occurred both before the Civil War (1861) and after it. Before the Civil War, the Blacks who attempted to free themselves of slavery were often caught and lynched. After the Civil War, some Whites too were lynched for opposing slavery of the Blacks. In each case of lynching, a man was first thrashed and then had to endure multiple fractures due to heavy beating and public humiliation before being hanged. It is estimated that there were around 2,400 lynching incidents in America between 1880 and 1930. In India though, lynching was unheard of until this century, although there were plenty of incidents of the mob attacking a thief or a rapist and giving him a sound thrashing in small town India. In the current spate of lynching, only the case of Mazloom Ansari and 12-year-old Imtiaz comes close to the American model; both the men were first attacked when they were moving with their livestock towards a cattle fair, walked some distance by their attackers even as they bled and groaned, and then hanged by a tree. In all other cases, the right-wing extremists charted a course, uniquely their own, which brings us to the dominant religious ideology being practised with unabashed grandeur in India since 2014. Our Constitution gives us Right to Equality and the State does not discriminate on the basis of religion, race, gender, caste

 Lynch Files

or creed. Yet in real life, the way things have panned out in recent years, it appears that there is only one way of being an Indian—everybody is supposed to eat the same stuff, speak the same language, and, maybe, even profess the same faith. For those who don't, there is clear 'othering'; the men and women whose *pitrabhoomi* (fatherland) and *punyabhoomi* (sacred land) are not the same, they are the ones to be marginalized; allowed to stay here only at the sweet will of the majority community, just as M. S. Golwalkar preached. In contemporary India, the establishment ideology legitimizes violence because of its innate belief in majoritarian or religious nationalism. Under this thumb rule, majority communalism is nationalism, and minority communalism is just communalism. This majoritarian nationalism is centred on the concept of violence, violence that is inflicted on 'others', and evolves a way of looking at them through a maze of hate, suspicion and condemnation. That is why, the Muslim for whom people in the past happily made space on a moving train to offer his prayers is today regarded with suspicion, almost like an alien, 'not people like us'. Today, the same Muslim's family members or friends call him not to offer prayers on train, or carry non-vegetarian biryani and kababs for the fear of being lynched as a beefeater. India is teetering on the brink.

We are witnesses too to an organized ideological apparatus—often perpetuated through toxic social media, hate speeches by all sorts of 'leaders' and open or latent support to this hate campaign by the ruling party—that spreads poison, generating a psychology of hatred and violence. With the success of each hate campaign, with the uploading of each lynching video, Mahatma Gandhi's India slips into greater danger.

Under the circumstances, the activism of the Supreme Court is welcome. Indeed, the court's proactive approach—for instance, it immediately admitted a petition on the Hapur lynching case after a private channel recorded the accused boasting of killing Qasim—could yet save the day for the nation. A new law to deal with lynching may be debatable, but it puts in black and white the punishment for the crime, and may force the assailants to think twice before they hunt for their new victim.

Lynching is not a temporary deviance from the normal, a departure from being a good society. It is the pathology of normalcy; the rot has entered into the deepest crevices of our society, and the blood stream of a sizable section of our population. For proof, one merely needs to see how the society and polity reacted to lynchings in Dadri and Una earlier and the more recent case of Rakbar in Alwar. Back in 2015, there was a sense of anger, betrayal and shock, as people bridged the distances and divide. There was even a 'Not in My Name' campaign by the common citizens keen to dissociate themselves from killings in the name of Hindutva. In 2016, the campaign attracted people across 16 cities and got prime space in the media. Men, women, even children gathered at Jantar Mantar and other public squares. They had nothing in common except their humanity and nationality. They were all outraged at this pubic cruelty towards others. When the same campaign was sought to be revived after Qasim's lynching in Hapur in 2018, the response was lukewarm at best. In other words, lynching was the new normal for many of us; it happened to 'others', not people like us.

Today, we have a section that is probably using cow slaughter as an excuse to settle age-old scores, to avenge the battles lost in ancient or medieval India. Today, men are being killed not because they killed a cow. They are being killed simply because they are Muslims and Dalits, again the two

communities said to be principal beefeaters of our society. And living as we do in times of dominant culture, it is just not acceptable to followers of dominant caste or religion. The soul of India is being challenged.

At one time, Golwalkar intended to use the vexed issue of cow slaughter to unite the country. Today, the same issue has driven a wedge down the middle. With each lynching incident, the chasm gets deeper. India stands divided.

As Harsh Mander wrote in *The Indian Express*:

> Muslims are today's castaways, today's political orphans with no home. This despite India being home to a tenth of world's Muslims, around 180 million people, making it the largest Muslim country after Indonesia and Pakistan. There has never been a harder time to be a Muslim in India, not since the stormy months that followed India's Partition. Today, the large majority of Muslims feel even more profoundly alone and abandoned. Open expressions of hatred and bigotry against Muslims have become the new normal, from schools to universities, workplaces to living rooms, internet to political rallies.[2]

Golwalkar's 'others' are reduced to almost aliens.

---

[2] 'Sonia, Sadly', *The Indian Express*, 24 March 2018.

Acknowledgements

To acknowledge the contribution of your near and dear ones towards the making of a book is well-nigh impossible. At the risk of sins of omission, I have to mention that this book would not have been possible, but for two individuals: Manisha Mathews, Executive Editor, Commissioning, SAGE, and Nadeem Khan of United against Hate. One afternoon, after a little discussion with my colleague Purnima Tripathi, I bounced off the idea to Manisha who did not take long in coming up with fresh suggestions to make *Lynch Files* not just a possibility but a more readable book, giving it a wider canvas than initially planned. Many thanks. Such a delight to work with you.

Similarly, when I shared the idea of the book with Nadeem bhai in the course of the promotion of *Of Saffron Flags and Skullcaps*, he readily agreed to share the details of some of the lynching victims, and a few of the photographs that appear in this book. As did brother Khaliquz Zaman, who displayed great alertness of mind to help me out at a crucial moment. I can never adequately thank John Dayal sahab for his generosity in sharing some of the photographs from his Karwaan-e-Mohabbat trip. Or, Mohammed Qumar Khan and Jaan Mohammed Sahab, who went out of their way to help me piece together the story of Akhlaq, the best known victim of lynching.

A word of gratitude is due to Dr Nirmala Lakshman, Director, *The Hindu*, and the author of the bestseller *Degree Coffee by the Yard: A Short Biography of Madras*. Also, I cannot be grateful enough for the spirit and wisdom of Professor Avijit Pathak of Jawaharlal Nehru University and Professor Mohammad Talib of University of Oxford, who made time for me on a rushed tour to India. Grateful! Also, I have to remember advocates Shadab Ansari sahab and Arif Ali sahab for their crucial inputs.

Not to forget my colleagues at *The Hindu* and *Frontline*. When I got bogged down, I could count on the support of R. Vijayasankar, Venkitesh Ramakrishnan, John Cherian, V. Venkatesan, Purnima Tripathi, T. S. Rajalakshmi and Divya Trivedi. Not to forget Jayanthi Krishnamachary and V. M. Rajasekhar in Chennai, both out of sight, but never short of a long-distance good word. Of course, a positive word at the right time from Anuj Kumar helped. As did that of Vijay Lokapally. They both read a section of the manuscript too. Then there was Anjana Rajan. Travelling across the United States, she still managed to squeeze out time to not only read a good part of the manuscript but also give valid suggestions. There are not many like her in the profession. Thanks to S. Ravi and Madhur Tankha too. As is inevitable with any such venture, my wife Uzma and kids, Maryam, Aliza, Juveria and Mishal, had to make allocations for my professional commitment and bear the demands on my time. Not to forget my nephews Osama Jalali and S. M. Umair and nieces Sana Khan and Rida Sadaqat, besides friends such as Aftab Alam, Mushtaq Ahmed, Masroor Mian, Rashid Ali, Aslam Khan, Irfan Ahmed and Mansoor Ansari. As I sign off, I cannot thank brother Khadim Hussain enough. In some prayers, I have his company, in others, his *dua*. May it stay that way!

File 1

Lynching

A SUBSTITUTE FOR COMMUNAL RIOTS

> In April 2017, *Huffington Post* reported, 'India was ranked fourth in the world in 2015—after Syria, Nigeria and Iraq—for the highest social hostilities involving religion'.

The findings barely created a ripple as the society was confronting a new expression of hate violence in the form of lynching. Riots, as a means of settling scores between religious communities, or even browbeating the minorities was passé. Instead, the society grappled with the menace of lynching. Since 2015, lynchings, not communal riots, have presented the biggest challenge to social cohesion, and in their derisive way, furthered the agenda of those who believe in one nation, one language, one food, one religion. Unsurprisingly, *IndiaSpend* found out in July 2018, barely a few days before Rakbar was killed by cow militia in Alwar on allegations of transporting cattle, 86 attacks fuelled by the suspicion of cow slaughter or beef consumption were reported from across the country since 2010. Of these, 98 per cent of the attacks occurred post May 2014, after the Bharatiya Janata Party (BJP) Government under Narendra Modi was sworn in.

> 'At least 33 persons were killed in these attacks—29 or 88% of whom were Muslim. Over 56% of all attacks occurred in states run by BJP governments'.

Incidentally, the *IndiaSpend* database of bovine-related hate crime was quoted by senior advocate Indira Jaising in her written submission to the Supreme Court to crack down on cow vigilantes.

Indeed, lynching has replaced the age-old communal riot as a means of polarization. Lynching comes without the burden of guilt that used to accompany riots. It is more effective, lethal and sinister. It strikes at the very identity of the community. It is far more demoralizing than the traditional communal violence, but serves the same purpose as riots did in the years gone by: to engender a climate of distrust and fear. On one side are Hindus who begin to look at any Muslim, particularly those with conspicuous manifestation of being one, with distrust. In their mind, all Muslims are beefeaters. And, maybe, even cow slaughterers. Nothing wrong with that if you are in Kerala, Tamil Nadu and vast stretches of the Northeast, but often a fatal flaw in north and west India. To those Hindus denied the benefit of education and economic cushion, a Muslim is one who deliberately provokes Hindus by eating beef. They do not know the reality or the history of beef eating in their own religion. For such a misled vigilante, the Muslim is the 'other' who must be shown his place. For him, a Muslim is what the latest video, real or fake, on WhatsApp shows him to be. Also, a Muslim is to be tackled, again, in the way those hooligans do in the lynching videos. That brings us to Muslims. With each lynching incident, the community slips deeper into fear, and into its own shell. And a community which is often told to join the mainstream slips further away.

In an item titled 'Black Shadow of the Mob' (*Times of India*, 29 July 2018), correspondent Himanshi Dhawan talked of how 'fear and alienation is changing the way middle-class Muslims live, from what they pack for lunch, to how they're naming babies'. The piece dwelt at some length on the perplex, insecure and increasingly insular world of a Muslim in urban India in 2018. It talked of well-known historian Rana Safvi's experience of living not too far from Dadri where Akhlaq was lynched soon after Eid-ul-Azha celebrations.

> One day, soon after Bakr-Id last year, when her relative came home with some mutton as a traditional gift, the watchman asked what was in the package, and the elderly gentleman told him. Safvi panicked. 'My house is close to Dadri, and I was overcome by this feeling of helplessness. What would I do if some men barged in demanding to know if it were beef in my fridge'.[3]

A year before this feature, the outgoing Vice President of India Hamid Ansari had stated in August 2017, 'Fear, unease is growing among Muslims in India'.[4] He was proved right exactly a year later when the same newspaper reported,

> Muslim traders in Ghansali town of Uttarakhand's Tehri Garhwal district said on Wednesday they are wary of opening their shops, two days after a man from their community was beaten up by a mob when he was found with a minor Hindu girl, sparking calls for their ouster.[5]

---

[3] 'Black Shadow of the Mob', *The Times of India*, 29 July 2018.
[4] 'Fear, Unease Growing among Muslims in India, says Outgoing Vice President Hamid Ansari', *Hindustan Times*, 10 August 2017.
[5] 'We are in Fear,' say Muslim Traders in Uttarakhand's Ghansali after Mob Violence', *Hindustan Times*, 1 August 2018.

Around the same time came another media report wherein young men and women in Delhi revealed that they call up their parents and grandparents not to offer namaz (prayer) on a train for the fear of being identified. This in a country where it was not unusual for people to make space for Muslim travellers to offer namaz as a train halted at the railway station, or even on the train itself. Writing in *The Wire*, Apoorvanand stated,

> A friend narrated his experience of offering namaz at the railway platform while waiting for his train. On earlier occasions, it had always been normal for him and others to pray in public. But this time, he was extra alert. A shout, a loud voice made him strain his ears. Was it for him? We who used to make space for namazis in train, in our homes, offices, and even offer a prayer mat to them have gone silent. Goondas have become our voice. This silence will drown India if we allow it to spread.[6]

All this fragmentation of our social fabric has come about not because of any major communal riot. In fact, since 2013, the country has not had any major outpouring of communal violence. It has come about because of the climate of fear, insecurity, vulnerability and helplessness generated by a series of lynching incidents. A lynching incident may take place in a remote town of Jharkhand or a busy town just off the NCR in Uttar Pradesh, but it comes laced with the potential to reach to millions across the country, particularly the Hindi heartland, through a video recording of the assault. Be it Akhlaq, or Samiuddin, Afrazul or Usman Ansari, all the incidents of attack

---

[6] Apoorvanand, 'Saying a Prayer for Our India, the Best Land in the World', *The Wire*, 13 May 2018.

on the minorities in the garb of cow slaughter have a ripple effect. Like a small piece of stone dropped into the sea, these cases of violence shake the entire community, from those in the immediate vicinity to the distant. Further, each attack polarizes the society while the police and state bodies can either go on dubbing each case as a minor aberration or completely deflect it as a mere road rage case.

A vast number of members of the majority, while appalled at the gruesome violence, somewhere justify it as 'he might have provoked it'. It is not too different in mindset from what the Uttar Pradesh Chief Minister Yogi Adityanath said after a particularly gruesome incident:

> Unnecessary importance is being given to lynching incidents. We will provide protection to everyone, but it is also the responsibility of every individual, every community and every religion to respect each others' sentiments. Humans are important and cows are important. Both have their own roles in nature.[7]

So subtly the blame is passed on to the victim. Much like the police which often files complaints against the attacked and the abused rather than the attackers and the abusers.

It is once again like the communal riots. Over the years, the Muslim community has had a grievance against the police that it favours the majority community—Hashimpura, Maliana, Bhagalpur, Bhiwadi, Moradabad and so on. It is the same with lynching incidents. Except for a solitary case of a police sub-inspector protecting a Muslim boy from a mob in Uttarakhand, the community lives with the uneasy feeling that even in case of murderous attack by cow vigilante groups, the police will

---

[7] 'Unnecessary Importance being given to Mob Lynching: UP CM Yogi Adityanath', *New Indian Express*, 25 July 2018.

come to the rescue of the offenders, find ways to protect the attackers and humiliate the victims. Again, like with communal riots, this time too, FIRs are filed against Muslims, some of them after they are killed by a murderous mob. Denied security in life by a rampant mob, they are denied dignity in death by the police.

Sadly, the effect of a lynching incident is more devastating than that of a riot. In the absence of a large-scale riot which almost always had casualties on both sides, the government and administration can claim to have provided peace and security to the masses yet there is a lingering fear of being next in the line. For instance, after the Gujarat pogrom of 2002, it took Muslims many years to come back to normal life. And even then, many people had to shift back to the ghettoes of the community for safety and security in case a riot recurred. Similarly, after lynching instances, Muslims of that area are immediately affected, and those beyond are indirectly affected. The immediately affected have to give up their age-old vocations of cattle rearing or dairy farming. Or, even leave the township or village forever. The distant ones suffer more subtly.

[
As reported by the media, people are being advised not to offer their prayer in public, not to eat beef even at home, not even to keep Muslim sounding names! Clearly, fear is the overriding consequence of lynching.
]

Much like it was when riots after riots used to take place. For proof, just take a walk around large parts of western

Lynch Files

Uttar Pradesh and meet men in their 20s with names such as Bheema Sheikh and Rahul Khan. These are the names of boys born after a series of riots in the Babri Masjid–Ram Janambhoomi movement. They are not names of a pluralist India at peace with its body and spirit. Rather, they are symbols of a community giving up its identity because of being gripped by a fear. So a name like Bheema, for a man almost into his 30s, is a safe one at the time of riots or lynching. He keeps his identity as a Sheikh, buys his security as a Bheema. Much like what Balraj Madhok, and later Murli Manohar Joshi, preached when they talked of assimilation of Muslims in the mainstream. They talked of names such as 'Muhammad Prasad' or 'Muhammad Kumar'. Those were the suggestions of a generation that had lived through communal riots, before, during and after the Partition. Today's lynching has already forced the families of Akhlaq, Alimuddin, Usman Ansari and others to shift to safer locales, maybe other vocations too. The change in name might just be the next step. If that happens, India's soul will be hurt by the onslaught on India's body.

Cow, a Sacred or a Political Animal?

Emboldened by the lynching incidents in Jharkhand and Rajasthan in 2016, unlettered *gau rakshaks* were turning on the heat in the name of the cow. That is when veteran historian D. N. Jha decided to put things into perspective. He said, '[cow vigilantes] have no love for the cow. Otherwise cows would not have been eating plastic at garbage dumps. They just hate the Muslims and the Dalits. The cow is just a political animal'. These words spoken in an interview with *Frontline* (17 August 2016) carried the simplicity of a common man yet came laced with the knowledge and profundity of a scholar who has spent a good part of half a century studying the evolution of the cow from a dietary preference and a sacred sacrificial offering to a political animal.

> The cow was never used for spiritual elevation. In 20th Century everybody used the cow as a political weapon. In the late 19th century and the early 20th century, Dayanand Saraswati used it for the mobilisation of Hindus. This even resulted in many Hindu-Muslim riots. Since 1925, the RSS [Rashtriya Swayamsewak Sangh] has used it in the same way. It has been used for politics, not just simple politics, but communal politics. It is an attempt at polarisation. The cow has nothing to do with the sacred or the spiritual. It is just a political animal.[8]

Asked about the RSS claim that before the coming of the Muslims, there was no cow slaughter, he scoffed at the contention, arguing,

> How can it say that? People have been eating beef all over. In Kerala, everybody eats beef, except the Namboodiris. Some 72 per cent of the communities eat beef. They have been doing so traditionally. In north-eastern India it is very common. The RSS does not know what is happening in this country. They say only Muslims and Dalits eat beef. It is all nonsense. If you go back in history, there is so much mention of cattle sacrifice and of cows being killed to propitiate deities. There is no doubt that cows were killed and that Brahmins ate cow meat. The practice continued even after the Vedic period. It existed during the Buddhist period and also during the time of the Mauryas. The Manu Smriti also mentions it. These fellows [Hindutva proponents] do not realise that the historical evidence is totally against

---

[8] 'The Cow is Just a Political Animal', *Frontline*, 2 September 2016.

Lynch Files

their viewpoint. Everybody knows that cows were killed on such occasions as marriage, the sacred thread ceremony, the arrival of the guest, at the time of death, at the time of house-warming. There are many instances listed in scriptures. If there was an honourable guest, he would be served cow meat. In agrarian societies it was very common. It took Brahmins a long time to change their outlook towards the cow. Later, much later, they gave up eating its meat. If you look at the Vedas or the Dharma Sutras, cow killing was fine. After the Mauryan period, references [to cow slaughter] become fewer and fewer in the texts. Towards the beginning of the first millennium A.D., this change was taking place, mainly in northern India.[9]

Indeed, the ill-informed communalists, the so-called *gau rakshaks* among them, who raise a hullabaloo over cow slaughter—at times, preferring to kill a man over a perceived or imagined intention to kill the cow—are not aware that beef eating has been a fairly popular practice in India, and even the scriptures speak in support. A historian like Jha gets the support of a scholar like H. H. Wilson, the first Chair of Sanskrit at Oxford.

Wilson wrote,

> The sacrifice of the horse or of the cow, the gomedha or ashvamedha, appears to have been common in the earlier periods of the Hindu ritual. Indian scholars like P.V. Kane and H.D. Sankalia who have been read by students at undergraduate level for half a century, too did not shy away from stating that cow flesh was part of diet in ancient India. Kane in *History of Dharmashastra*

---

[9] 'The Cow is Just a Political Animal', *Frontline*, 2 September 2016.

referred to Vedic passages which talk of cow killing and beef eating. Similarly, Sankalia put together archaeological evidence of cow flesh being part of the diet in ancient India.[10]

Jha himself gave an exhaustive account of Hindu deities and their preference for cattle flesh, either as part of their food or as part of a sacrifice to propitiate them in *The Myth of the Holy Cow* as also *Against the Grain*. In the latter, he wrote, 'Unlike the licentious Indra, Agni drank soma moderately, his main food being ghee. He is described as "one whose food is the ox and the barren cow," but ashva, bulls (rishabhha), oxen (ukshana), barren cows (vasa) and rams (mesha) were also sacrificed for him'.

Similarly, the Shatapatha Brahmana talks of 'sterile spotted cow' being offered to Maruts. Taittiriya Brahmana goes one step further, mentioning that the cow 'is verily food'. The Gopatha Brahmana gives details of the division of a cow carcass. It recommends 36 shares by the Samitara who killed the victim by strangulation. The Brahmanas also talk of the use of cowhide in domestic rituals such as the parting of the hair during pregnancy or investiture ceremony.

[The Mahabharata too refers to well-respected king Rantideva. He was a man 'in whose kitchen two thousand cows were butchered each day, their flesh, along with grain, being distributed among the Brahmanas'.]

---

[10] 'On Beef Eating in Ancient India', *Merinews*, 1 April 2008, available at: http://www.merinews.com/article/on-beef-eating-in-ancient-india/131750.shtml

As Jha himself says, 'It is significant that out of 250 animals mentioned in the Vedas, 50 were considered fit for sacrifice and for eating'. The humble cow was among those found fit for both sacrifice and eating. Indeed, in ancient India, serving the cow meat to a special guest was considered the right thing to do, much like a person from the lower-income group does today with mutton. Today, a person who cannot afford goat or lamb meat goes for beef. However, on a special occasion or the arrival of an important guest, mutton is served to the guest. During the Vedic Age, it was the other way round, with cow meat being served to special guests as a mark of honour.

So how and when did the cow come to be infused with a halo? The process began during the time of the Mauryas. It gained some traction towards the end of the ancient India period. However, it continued to be part of the diet. It was during the Mughal Age that a definite move towards safeguarding cattle was made. Part of the reason was the cattle population was dwindling and they were necessary for many Hindu rituals. It will be appropriate to remember that in ancient India often the priests were paid in cattle for their services. However, all along, the cow was an innocent animal, part of the diet in south and east India, part of sacrifice in north India. It was after the failure of the Revolt of 1857 that the cow came to occupy important space in the life of a Hindu, at least in north India.

From the mid-1870s, demands were made to prohibit cow slaughter. *Gaurakshini sabhas* came into being. Starting with Punjab, they spread to Gujarat, even Awadh. Incidentally, the first foes for *gaurakshini sabhas* were not Muslims but the British, whom they held responsible for slaughtering cows for their kitchen on a regular basis. It was only in the early years of the twentieth century that *gaurakshini sabhas* focussed on Muslims as possible perpetrators of cow slaughter. That is when the cow protection movement came to develop communal hues, and noises to ban cow slaughter became shrill. So much so that various Hindu organizations like the RSS started regarding the Muslims, and not the British, as their prime enemies. Amazingly, V. D. Savarkar did not raise his voice against cow slaughter, and in an even more shocking development, Swami Vivekananda recommended beef eating as the easiest way to develop a muscular, energetic society.

After the Partition though, this teaching of Vivekananda was forgotten, as was Savarkar's opposition to regarding the cow as a sacred animal. Instead, the Jana Sangh started a long drawn out anti-Muslim campaign which focussed on the cow as a mother (*mata*), and with increasing vigour prevailed upon many state assemblies in independent India to ban cow slaughter.

Today, the animal is used to marginalize both Muslims and Dalits: the former being lynched for transporting the animal, the latter for skinning the dead cows. The Muslims and Dalits find themselves on the same side of the divide, much against the situation in medieval India, when well-off Muslims would prefer mutton, and poorer sections of Hindus and Muslims often made do with beef.

The murder of Akhlaq, the stripping and thrashing of the victims in Una are public statements of men who have forgotten their own history. Had the killers of Akhlaq or the perpetrators of torture in Una read their history rather than listening to their neighbourhood party president, things would have been entirely different.

The Oft-present Political Hand

He was an alumnus of the Indian Institute of Technology, which spells 'cream'. He was educated at Harvard too. He worked at McKinsey, and was widely regarded as one of the liberal,

urbane faces of the ruling dispensation. Even those who disagreed with Jayant Sinha's politics never read an element of bigotry into his actions. Indeed, amid a sea of foaming-at-the-mouth rabble-rousers in his party, he seemed the most acceptable figure to an educated Indian. Then Sinha did the unthinkable. He provided legal assistance to and financed the court cases of the 11 men held for the murder of Alimuddin in Ramgarh in Jharkhand. He had a fig leaf of an excuse then: The men were merely accused, not convicted of the crime.

It was later, after their conviction, when Sinha garlanded eight of them on their being released on bail, that all hell broke loose. Here was a union minister, supposedly the more benign face of the ruling party, garlanding those convicted of lynching a Muslim citizen to death. Even as Sinha clarified he was merely 'honouring the due process of law' and claimed to 'unequivocally condemn all acts of violence and reject any type of vigilantism', the damage was done.

The photograph of the convicts standing with Sinha at his residence with marigold garlands around their necks and a box of sweets to complete the occasion, said it all. And Sinha, who claimed he had provided legal assistance to the accused because they were from his constituency, was deprived of this excuse too when it was revealed that he had never visited the widow of Alimuddin, who too is a citizen of his constituency. Harvard seemed such a distant memory that when somebody suggested that Harvard take away Sinha's degree, it served to drive home the message: Bigotry is not susceptible to education. And lynch mobs come with a political blessing, a ubiquitous hand of support.

Call it political patronage for the crime, but there is no denying that behind almost every lynching incident, there have been leaders of a political party to lend the accused a shoulder, to guide them, to pick them up if they were to stumble or fail, and to fire salvos at the victims with such audacity that the victims, at times, appeared villains.

For all his cloak of an intellectual, Sinha's words were no different in impact from those of fellow BJP leader Sangeet Som who asked for Akhlaq's family to be jailed for allegedly killing a calf! That the family had lost its senior male member to a mob attack did not deter Som from issuing another brazen warning that smacked of a complete disregard for the law and the constitution: 'They should not forget Muzaffarnagar', he said as he continued his diatribe from the same temple from which the fatal announcement of a calf being killed had been made. Muzaffarnagar, it may be recalled, presented one of the worst cases of communal violence in 2013 between landed Jats and poor Muslims in which the poorer section suffered at the hands of the landowners.

Sinha's hand, at least in part, was pushed by the fact that fellow BJP leaders in Jharkhand were raking in all the credit for the bail of the convicts. Earlier, other local leaders had helped take out a rally of nearly 30,000 people in support of Alimuddin's murderers. Former MLA Shankar Chaudhary had led the marchers asking for a Central Bureau of Investigation (CBI) enquiry into the incident after a local court pronounced life imprisonment to the 11 men found guilty of murdering Alimuddin. In the political crucible, Sinha had to beat them at their own game. The felicitation of the convicts was an easy dice to roll. It was competing communalism. Alimuddin and justice to his family was but collateral damage.

Coming back to Som, he too was upstaged in this sordid game by his party colleague Mahesh Sharma in the Dadri lynching. Immediately after Akhlaq was murdered, Som said his bit and departed. Mahesh Sharma proved a more resilient supporter of the killers. After meekly advising Akhlaq's family to treat his killing as a mere *haadsa* (an accident), he came back when a local man accused of killing Akhlaq died, allegedly of dengue. This time, he came as a loving father figure, a doting adult who had lost a loved younger one, and wrapped the body of the accused in the Tricolour to send him on his last journey.

Incidentally, like Sinha, Sharma is a well-read man. For years, he has been a practising doctor. Back in the mid-1990s, when Narendra Modi was not on the horizon, he got Atal Bihari Vajpayee and L. K. Advani to bless him at the inauguration of Kailash Hospital which he built in Noida. The hospital, named after his father, marked a major landmark in Sharma's journey that had started from a humble lower-middle-income group flat in Noida's Sector 19 and regular attendance at local RSS Shakhas. From a two-room flat to residence in the decidedly upmarket Sector 15A in Noida, Sharma had come a long way. He, unlike Sinha, had not forgotten his early grooming. So he made his presence felt by wrapping the body of a murder accused in the Tricolour. He felt emboldened too to give a certificate of nationalism to late President A. P. J. Abdul Kalam, calling him 'a nationalist despite being a Muslim'. The rest just fell into place.

The suave Sinha and the upwardly mobile Sharma have the company of the elegant Vasundhara Raje Scindia who chose to dignify the murder of Pehlu Khan with rehearsed silence for a month. Her quiet was broken only when 23 former IAS officers wrote an open letter condemning the incident,

> We are very disturbed by the lynching and murder of Pehlu Khan in Alwar. We are also dismayed by the acts of omission and commission by the government

following the incident, including the delay and marked reluctance in arresting all those guilty of the act.[11]

Scindia responded by vowing not to tolerate any acts of intolerance in the state. Her words were obviously not heeded, because soon after Pehlu, Umar was lynched in Rajasthan, followed about a year later by Rakbar's lynching, again in Alwar. Among those who turned a deaf ear to Scindia's belated proclamation was Gyan Dev Ahuja, her own party MLA, who raised his voice for the release of the men accused of lynching Rakbar. He did not confine himself to the 'innocent till proven guilty' routine. Instead, he asked the police to nab Aslam too.

Aslam, incidentally, was the man fortunate enough to escape the violent villagers as they laid their hands on Rakbar. Ahuja later stated, 'Cow slaughtering is a bigger crime than terrorism. Terrorists kills two-three people. Cow slaughtering (sic) hurt the sentiments of crores of Hindus'.

Amid these wars of declaration and declamation, the political predilection of the accused became clearer with each episode, just as the preference of the political bosses shone brighter with each lynching. Not surprisingly, most of the lynching incidents have taken place in the BJP-ruled states. Even less surprising have been the attempts by the BJP leaders to come to the rescue of the men accused of lynching. It is a given with their Hindutva politics wherein every non-Hindu is considered a second-grade citizen whose life, honour, employment, depends on consistent good behaviour, and periodic renewal of his patriotism certificate by self-styled Hindutva hawks masquerading as nationalists. Their core vote bank expects that, and the politicians deliver without fail.

---

[11] 'Justice for Pehlu Khan: Former Rajasthan IAS Officers Write to CM Vasundhara Raje Demanding Probe', *India Today*, 24 April 2017.

Lynch Files

This again was in keeping with the age-old politics of vote banks that the country suffers from. The politics of vote banks has become inseparable from India's brand of democracy. Caste, community, religion, gender, economics, any element of division can lend itself to vote banks. All parties without exception have used this situation, and the ruling dispensation has made a trophy out of it. The despicable term 'appeasement' as a blanket condemnation of social justice attempts stems from this perspective the politicians have of looking at the voting public. If justice is served to the minorities, or even to the weakened majority traditionally oppressed, then the opposing vote banks will be affected.

No wonder, Akhlaq's brother, Jaan Mohammed, complained that the prime minister did not even issue the customary message of condolence at the death of Akhlaq. Nor did any help come the way of the family. Instead, the men accused of killing him were helped with jobs after being granted bail.

As reported by *The Hindu*,

> Fifteen of the youths accused of lynching Mohammad Akhlaq in Bishara village of Dadri in September 2015 over suspicion of storing beef in his house have landed contractual jobs with NTPC Limited. Tejpal Nagar, the local BJP MLA, facilitated their recruitment in a meeting with senior NTPC officials.[12]

The spokesman of the National Thermal Power Corporation (NTPC) though insisted,

> Yes, we have agreed to give jobs to unemployed youths of Bishara. It has nothing to do with Akhlaq's lynching. Contractual jobs have been offered to many

---

[12] 'Dadri Accused get Contractual Jobs at NTPC', *The Hindu*, 14 October 2017.

residents of Bishara because it is the NTPC's policy to give jobs to all project-affected persons based on their qualification and expertise.[13]

The alleged job availability, however, was not the worst piece of news to come from the area. It came from Hapur some two and a half years after Akhlaq had been done to death.

In the busy western Uttar Pradesh township, Qasim was assaulted and dragged to death even as the camera captured it all live, while Samiuddin was thrashed, abused and kicked badly enough to land up in the ICU of a local hospital. However, the local bar association, in a chilling replay of Ashifa's case in Jammu—the 8-year-old girl was gang raped but the local bar association raised its voice for the accused men—sided with the accused. The Hapur Bar Association argued that the two men arrested by the police were innocent and were being persecuted by the police. They demanded that they be set free immediately or else the Bar would have to launch a massive public stir to secure their release.

The Bar's decision was hailed by the township's BJP leaders, who too insisted that cow killers had been lynched, and if the men were innocent, the law would declare them so. The facile argument was very much like the stand taken by some lawyers and right-wing Hindutva group protestors in Rajsamand after Afrazul had been mutilated and burnt to death allegedly by Shambhu Lal. They too claimed he was innocent. While denouncing the dastardly act, they insisted that if Afrazul were innocent of the crime he was said to have committed, he would come out unscathed in any legal battle. It struck them not, that fire had already consumed Afrazul.

The dead do not come back. Even political brinkmanship has its limitations.

---

[13] 'Dadri Accused get Contractual Jobs at NTPC', *The Hindu*, 14 October 2017.

COMMON MAXIMUM PROGRAMME: SIMILARITIES IN LYNCHING INCIDENTS

Much before India kept its tryst with destiny in 1947, Hindutva ideologue M. S. Golwalkar had outlined the place of the minorities in the country in his much talked about *We, or Our Nationhood Defined*. Golwalkar wrote,

> There are only two courses open to these foreign elements *(Muslims and Christians)*, either to merge themselves in the national race and adopt its culture or to live at its mercy so long as the national race may allow them to do so and quit the country at the sweet will of the national race. That is the only sound view on the minorities' problem... [The] foreign races in Hindustan must either adopt the Hindu culture and language, must learn to respect and hold in reverence Hindu religion, must entertain no idea but those of the glorification of the Hindu race and culture, i.e., of the Hindu nation and must lose their separate existence to merge in the Hindu race, or may stay in the country, wholly subordinated to the Hindu Nation, claiming nothing, deserving no privileges, far less any preferential treatment—not even citizen's rights.[14]

---

[14] M. S. Golwalkar, 1939, *We, or Our Nationhood Defined*, Bharat Publications, Nagpur.

For many decades after he penned these words, the proponents of Hindutva were wary of quoting passages from the book in public. Indeed, even the ruling BJP hardly made a reference to Golwalkar's words when Atal Bihari Vajpayee was the prime minister. Things changed in 2014. First, Prime Minister Narendra Modi evoked Deendayal Upadhyaya, another Hindutva ideologue, in advising his party men, 'Do not rebuke Muslims. Do not reward Muslims. Assimilate them'. It was but a euphemism for Golwalkar's more candid expression about the minorities having to lose their own identity if they had to survive in India.

Now, unfortunately, the second part of Golwalkar's advice is being implemented, word by word, thought by thought, action by action. Through the unending series of lynching instances, beginning 28 September 2015 and continuing until present, the Muslims, and to a lesser extent, the Dalits, are being told that they are here at the mercy of the majority community. That they can claim no rights, no privileges, not even equal footing. Much like what Golwalkar wrote,

> [F]oreign races in Hindustan must ... learn to respect and hold in reverence Hindu religion ... and must lose their separate existence to merge in the Hindu race, or may stay in the country, wholly subordinated to the Hindu Nation, claiming nothing, deserving no privileges, far less any preferential treatment—not even citizen's rights.[15]

A dispassionate look at all the lynching incidents proves that none of them is a spontaneous action of unlettered albeit headstrong villagers whose religious sentiments have been hurt, but a well thought out action with specific victims

---

[15] Golwalkar, 1939, *We, or Our Nationhood Defined*.

in mind. The cow is held as a sacred animal by a section of Hindus. But in the cases of lynching, it becomes a political animal with which to browbeat and even murder the minorities and the Dalits. Remember what well-known activist Bezwada Wilson had to say about Dalits being forced to remove the cattle carcass? 'When the cow is alive, she is the mother of the Brahmins. When dead, why does it become the responsibility of the Dalits to dispose off the body?'

The modus operandi in lynching cases remains the same, the 'common maximum programme' almost identical. In almost all cases, it starts with unproven allegations of cow smuggling or cow slaughter. The presence of cattle on a truck is taken as a proof of smuggling. Similarly, the presence of a carcass of the animal is regarded as evidence of the animal having been killed by either a Muslim or a Dalit. That the man transporting the cows, as in Delhi or Alwar, has all the valid documents showing purchase of the animal from a cattle fair is not held as a sound enough reason to avoid the cold-blooded murder of the innocent. Even a point as elementary as the man accused of cow smuggling or slaughter being a dairy farmer by profession is never regarded as a sufficient ground to stay off him. That he and his ancestors had been milk vendors for decades matters not a bit to a mob short of both education and common sense. Even the clear market mantra that while the milch cow with which the men have been held costs anything between ₹25,000 and ₹45,000, selling the same to a butcher, or even killing it on one's own, fetches only ₹6,000 or so, fails to register with the bloodthirsty mob.

Importantly, during the past three years or so, no major instance of lynching has taken place where a Hindu dairy farmer or transporter was a victim. Even in cases when a truck or tempo was being driven by a Hindu man, he is allowed to go, while the Muslim dairy farmers are assaulted, and finally killed. Being a Muslim is to invite murder, being a Hindu is to have a safety halo around you in the parlance of *gau rakshaks*, who are actually just murderers or extortionists.

In all the cases, after the victim is badly beaten, bruised and almost killed, the cows are confiscated. This happens despite valid documents of their purchase and transport. The animals are sent to a cow shelter and not to the victim's family, in a clear indictment of the victim. So the victim loses his life, his family loses both the breadwinner and the means to earn their daily bread. It was the same with Mazloom Ansari in Jharkhand. It was the same with Pehlu Khan in Alwar, and the same with Satna victims in Madhya Pradesh.

The confiscation of the cattle begins a cycle of further harassment of the victims and their kith and kin. Often, the police files an FIR against the dead for cow smuggling.

Muslim dairy farmers are all addressed as cow smugglers in the first address to the press after the incident. Never once does the police assume that the innocent men may have been waylaid by thugs on the road, deprived of their legal earnings, looted and killed. The electronic media too is happy to call them smugglers. The reality is, in all the cases, the men who pay with their life for somebody practising Golwalkar's advice are first looted, then murdered. Worse, they are denied dignity in death with the police labelling them as *gau taskar* in Hindi or 'cow smugglers' in English. How the police comes to a conclusion even before an elementary investigation is never explained. Nor is a case registered about the cattle theft of the deceased.

The expression finds home in the mind of the common man. A Muslim has to be a smuggler. He cannot be a law-abiding

dairy farmer who looks after his cows, his buffaloes and the bulls. He has to be a butcher, bringing the animals on the sly, not a man of dignity procuring the animals from an open market with all the receipts.

Then begins the next stage of trouble for the affected family. Lawyers have to be engaged to clear the name of the departed. In some cases, the companions, the fellow travellers of the departed are accused too of 'smuggling' and/or 'slaughter'. The police files an FIR against the injured, and waits for the badly mauled men to recover in hospital before arresting them.

In some cases, when the police does not arrest the survivor, local BJP leaders call for arrest, forcing the man to go into hiding, depriving him further of his livelihood, and family, until he is finally given a clean chit. Interestingly, while the police seldom refrains from referring to the victims as smugglers, there is always an attempt made to protect the assailants.

It all starts with an attempt to sidestep the core issue. For instance, in Hapur, the police was at pains to call it a case of road rage where two bikes collided on the road, leading to an altercation between the affected men. That no bikes were discovered, no accident was reported, mattered not a bit. It needed the guilty men to upload a video of their action for the police to change tack.

In the case of Junaid in Ballabhgarh, the police tried to underplay the incident as a trivial fight over a seat on the train. The attempt is to deny the obvious and confuse the common man about the sinister design at work.

Similarly, in the Rakbar case, the police, instead of rushing the victim to the hospital to improve his chances of survival,

drove around the town for three hours, deposited his cows at a shelter, and had a cup of tea, before finally reaching the community health centre. Initial attempts were to portray it as a case of trespassing where the villagers caught the men who were trespassing through their fields under the cover of darkness. Later, the police arrested three men, two of whom had helped take the victim to the hospital. Who was protected, who was made a scapegoat, who was the culprit was not known.

Of course, in the much-publicized case of Akhlaq in Dadri, a case of cow slaughter was filed against the deceased, and his family. That this was against all norms of justice did not alter the course of the case. A family which had lost its patriarchal head and had one of the sons undergo serious brain surgeries was saddled with the responsibility of proving its innocence. Earlier, its privacy had been intruded upon both by the police and the murderers. The mob laid hands on the victim sleeping in his bedroom; the police raided his home refrigerator. The priest who allegedly made the announcement over a microphone at the temple about a calf being killed escaped.

The pattern of socio-economic exclusion of the victims continues. A little after the FIRs are filed, and sundry arrests made, the victim family is asked by the local Hindu residents to take back the court case filed against the attackers if they want to go back to their house. Usman Ansari, who was almost burnt by the mob, wanted to go back home but was denied the chance by his fellow villagers, who wanted him to withdraw the case he had filed against some of them before setting foot in his own house. Alimuddin's family was reduced to a pariah, and Akhlaq's family left the village forever. In fact, they had to leave the town, the state too. One of his brothers settled on the Delhi border, his own sons shifted to Delhi.

Again, this movement of the victims from their place of residence to another place goes unregistered in the media, and is of no avail to the larger society. The message is clear: 'They have had to hide their faces after what they had done. So they have shifted'. There never is an introspection as to why a family that had lived with people of other religions for decades without complaint had to leave home and hearth and begin life afresh elsewhere. It reinforces, yet again, Golwalkar's argument of the minorities being there at the whims and sweet will of the majority.

Even as the bereaved look for other places for their safety, the perpetrators of the assault are emboldened to go public with their deed. They make videos of their heinous crimes and upload them online. In most cases, one of the young men records the attack on the unarmed victim. In the case of Afrazul in Rajasthan, it was a 14-year-old child who was brainwashed into recording the macabre killing. The videos are widely circulated through WhatsApp, reaching the poor and unlettered too. That they may lack the ability to differentiate between truth and falsehood is immaterial.

In some cases, as in Afrazul, the brutality is recorded in detail, and the action celebrated to the last second. Much like Akhlaq's blood-splattered face next to the assailants' feet. In others, as in Samiuddin, the beard is pulled, the man is spat at, abused. All on camera. The idea is to intimidate him, and those who identify with him in faith. Or, take the case of Alimuddin, where the victim's face is lifted by the attackers to present a clear view to the camera. He is the trophy for rampant practitioners of virulent Hindutva. The pacific cow is far from the mind, and from the picture.

The video attracts millions of eyeballs. It is raised to a work of cinema, the murder of the innocent portrayed as a spectacle

File 1: Lynching

to be devoured. The victim is projected like a helpless villain cornered at the end by the aggressive hero. The kicks, the butts, the slaps, the blood, the gore, all presented unabashedly, without a single cut. The word spreads: 'A Muslim cow killer has been finished off!' The friends and community of the attackers feel jubilant at their accomplishment, religion and its misrepresentation acting as a collective 'opium of the masses'. The victim's community, meanwhile, sinks into despair. There is no sense of safety and security. The message to all Muslims is the same: You could be the next one. Just as Golwalkar would have liked.

Gaurakshini Sabhas: Walk Down to the Nineteenth Century

The movement against cow slaughter while not exactly rooted in antiquity is almost 150-year old. Soon after 1857, the movement began to take root. It initially began as an anti-British movement. Back then, the focus was on the British who were said to slaughter cows daily for their kitchen. Amazingly, some Muslims too were part of the movement then. Authors Dharampal and T. M. Mukundan said it all in *British Origin of Cow Slaughter in India*. They wrote,

> The enormity of the movement and the threat it posed to the British may be gauged by the statement of Viceroy Lansdowne when he said that: 'I doubt whether, since the Mutiny, any movement containing in it a greater amount of potential mischief has engaged the attention of the Government of India'. They point out that a huge number of cattle were slaughtered daily by the British for their army and civilian personnel in India, yet very little is known, even to most scholars and historical researchers on India, about this India-wide Anti-Kine-Killing Movement against the British during

1880–1894. Even the scholars who have taken note of this movement have treated it as a Hindu–Muslim conflict. But such was not the case, as many Muslims as well as the Parsis and Sikhs actively participated in the movement. The fact that the movement was directed against the British and not against the Muslims, as commonly believed, was clear to Queen Victoria and her officers. Queen Victoria said in a letter to Viceroy Lord Lansdowne, 'Though the Muhammadan's cow killing is made the pretext for the agitation, it is, in fact, directed against us, who kill far more cows for our army, etc., than the Muhammadans'. Faced with a challenge, the British did what they were best at: divide and rule. They soon spread the rumour that the Muslims were cow-eaters, and ably turned what was a political movement against the British into a communal issue between the two leading communities.[16]

The British task was facilitated by some members of the Marwari community who came to regard Muslims as their prime enemies while seeking support of tradition for some of their actions. For instance, cows were actively linked to Shri Krishna in the early years of the twentieth century. Hardly a surprise, the Yadavas, who were worshippers of the cow, came to play an important role in the nascent cow protection movement. The Yadavas' love for the cow was bankrolled by the moneyed Marwari community; they had the financial wherewithal, but were looking for greater social respect. Funding the cow protection movement came in as a fine opportunity. Writing in *Gita Press and the Making of Hindu India*, Akshaya Mukul said,

---

[16] Dharampal and T. M. Mukundan, 2002, *British Origin of Cow Slaughter in India*, Society for Integrated Development of Himalayas, Uttarakhand.

The later decades of the nineteenth century and the early ones of the twentieth were a time of rising religious antagonism between Indus and Muslims, marked by frequent riots and competitive communalism. Besides the battle for supremacy between Hindi and Urdu, incidents of cow slaughter and music before mosques were becoming flashpoints between the two communities— from the major riot of 1893 in Azamgarh, Mau and adjoining areas on the issue of cow slaughter during Bakr-Id, to the resurgence of widespread violence in 1917 in Bihar's Shahabad, Gaya and Patna.[17]

In the last two decades of the nineteenth century, nascent steps were taken towards starting a cow protection movement. The beginning was made by Dayanand Saraswati with the publication of the pamphlet *Gaukarnidhi*, in 1881. As he travelled across north India, from Punjab to Uttar Pradesh, he was able to set up *gaushalas* and *gaurakshini sabhas* and *samitis*. This grassroots mass contact programme changed the composition of the movement from being a multi-religious movement seeking a ban on cow slaughter for economic reasons to a religious one where the proponents often got into direct confrontation with the Muslims and Dalits, perceived to be the principal consumers of cow meat. Communal riots were not long in the coming. In early 1890s, first riots on the issue of cow were reported. The first incident of violence came from Bombay where Gau Rakshak Mandali's proactive and allegedly provocative actions, aimed at othering the Muslims, led to riots in Bombay Presidency towards the end of 1982.

The movement continued to gain ascendancy. Indeed as early as 1923 cow protection movement activists had made inroads

---

[17] Akshaya Mukul, 2015, *Gita Press and the Making of Hindu India*, Harper Collins, New Delhi.

into the Congress, then spearheading the national movement. If the Hindu Mahasabha and Arya Samaj came together to make common cause on cow slaughter, leaders such as Madan Mohan Malviya, Lala Lajpat Rai and Rajendra Prasad forced the party to tackle the volatile issue. The Hindu Mahasabha started timing its annual sessions to coincide with those of the Congress, thus forcing the grand old party of the freedom movement to take a stand in favour of cow protection. By this time, the cow protection movement had gained ascendancy with the setting up of many *gaurakshini sabhas*, *gau rakshak mandals*, and even *gau sewak* newspapers. The movement shunned its anti-colonial past completely; the Muslims too withdrew from it totally. Not surprisingly, the movement became totally hostile to Muslims, giving rise to frequent tension between the communities in north India. Due to this, 91 riots were reported from the United Provinces. By the time India kept its destiny with freedom, *gau raksha* activists were talking of giving the animal the status of a national animal and banning its slaughter. They met with success too, however, limited. Although slaughter was not banned, the state was encouraged to frame laws in this direction. Through Article 48 of the Constitution's section on Directive Principles of State Policy, cow slaughter found its mention in the law book of the nation. Although Directive Principles are not justiciable or necessarily enforceable, the very mention of cow slaughter in this section proved that the activists had made themselves heard in the right quarters. And on some unspecified date in future, the same was to have the force of law. Taking the clue, the states of Rajasthan, Uttar Pradesh, Madhya Pradesh and Bihar passed laws against cow slaughter.

Not much later, in independent India the cow became a political animal, and cow protection movement gained in pace and popularity. M. S. Golwalkar, the guru of Hindutva movement, was the brain behind the movement for around 20 years after Independence. He demanded that a nationwide ban be imposed on cow slaughter, and the government responded by setting up a committee to deliberate on the demand. Golwalkar was on the committee. He went around the country to collect a million signatures for his anti-cow killing petition. As part of the signature drive, he went to a village in Uttar Pradesh where he saw a woman in a village who went from house to house to get more signatures. To his fellow committee member Verghese Kurien, Golwalkar said,

> This is when I realized that the woman was actually doing it for her cow, which was her bread and butter, and I realized how much potential the cow has. I saw that the cow has potential to unify the country—she symbolizes the culture of Bharat. You agree with me to ban cow slaughter on this committee and I promise you, five years from that date, I will have united the country. What I'm trying to tell you is that I'm not a fool, I'm not a fanatic. I'm just cold-blooded about this. I want to use the cow to bring out our Indianness.[18]

Of course, in 1966, various outfits pledged their support for cow protection, and sat on a dharna at the Parliament. For a few decades, the issue went on the backburner, as the Hindutva forces sought to unite the Hindu community behind its demand for building a Ram Mandir in Ayodhya. However, as the Mandir movement began to peter out, the Gujarat Chief Minister Narendra Modi was quick to talk of a Pink Revolution and started a campaign against buffalo meat in 2009. Some three years later, Bhartiya Gau Raksha Dal (BGRD) came into being. Followed only three years later with the lynching of Mohammed

---

[18] Verghese Kurien, 2008, *I Too Had a Dream*, Roli Books, New Delhi.

Lynch Files

Akhlaq in Dadri on mere suspicion of storing beef in his fridge. The days of 'othering' of Muslims, which began with the initial works of Dayanand Saraswati, were over. The days of elimination of Muslims for mere possession or transportation of cattle had taken over, and *gau raksha dals* delivered what they believe to be instant 'justice' on the road. No hearing, no case, no court. Just instant punishment for those supposed to be guilty.

Bhartiya Gau Raksha Dal: Part-time Professionals

> We have so many affiliates. People join us for some time, and go away. Some work independently. Mostly, people work as a gau rakshak on a part-time basis. It is not like if one works as a gau rakshak, he will become Narendra Modi in 10 years or Amit Shah. It is not politics. Most gau rakshaks have other occupations. Some are engineers, some are artists, some teachers. They become gau rakshaks out of their love for gau mata. They work with us on a part-time basis. But I must concede that over the past few years, some have worked only for a few days as a gau rakshak, then gone as a volunteer to work with the BJP at the time of elections. At times, they join that political party. If some person does that, we take action against him. We expel from Bhartiya Gau Raksha Dal. (Interview with the author)

These are the words of Pawan Pandit, founder of BGRD which, he claims, has a task force of 6,000 volunteers. It is claimed to be a protection force, never mind that the cow's head on its emblem is flanked by two men wielding AK47!

Everything about the work of a *gau rakshak*, according to him, is fine, pacific and sacred. People join out of a sense of reverence for the cow as a mother. The emblem too states,

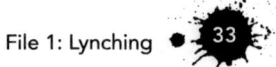

File 1: Lynching 33

'Gau Mataram' (cow is mother). But then, how does this love disappear when the scent of political victory floats in the air? He refuses to answer, except reiterating that *gau raksha* (cow protection) is not a get-rich-fast career option. Oh, never mind all the rescued cattle, all the gaushalas with their attendant pecuniary spin-offs.

> *Gau raksha*, to him, means a long, sleepless night, standing on forsaken roads, waiting for a truck with smuggled cattle to arrive. The truck may never come or may come just once or twice in a week. The self-appointed protectors of the cow though have to be on a vigil. But it is not their job. There is police to catch the thieves or to send the rescued animals to cow shelters. But these *gau rakshaks*, high on the opium of religion, think nothing of taking the law into their hands.

The police as a law-abiding force has its limitations. The *gau rakshaks*, openly working despite the law, not because of the law or with it, have no such compunctions. One sight of a cow smuggler, preferably a Muslim, and they swing into action. Lathis, batons, swords, belts, hockey sticks, even cricket bats, anything they can lay their hands on, is used to administer an instant dose of street violence to the man accused of smuggling cattle. The victim may have his papers in order. He may have paid the toll tax at previous checkpoint. But, to self-proclaimed *gau rakshaks*, these are just pieces of paper.

The police palms can be greased too. The papers can be fake. It is only the *gau rakshaks* who are overboard. It is a world where no law applies. Or, at least, that is how they behave.

There is a mushrooming of *gau raksha dals* in recent times. In Gujarat alone, as many as 200 cow vigilante groups have sprung up.[19]

Also in an interview with *Live Mint*, he is reported to have said, 'Some just use our name to take revenge over issues that have nothing to do with cow protection. Ask most of them if they have ever done *gau daan*. How many cows do they have in their houses? Am sure no one does'.[20]

The *gau rakshaks* work as a team with one group alerting others on mobile on the slightest suspicion of cow smugglers reaching a spot. Within minutes, a group gathers at the next checkpoint. Thus the nights are spent. Days are for their other jobs. Some, as Pandit claims, are engineers, some are teachers. Some are farmers. Some are simply students. That is by day. Cometh the dusk, cometh their avatar of a *gau rakshak*.

Based in Delhi, Pandit coordinates the work of BGRD volunteers across India, but concentrates on Punjab, Rajasthan, Haryana, Gujarat and Uttar Pradesh. There are offices in places such as Maharashtra, Goa and Andhra Pradesh as well. 'If somebody is doing cattle smuggling in, say, Bengal, or Bihar, we do not have our volunteers there. So we cannot act, but we do have our affiliates. Our forces work in mostly Haryana, UP and other neighbouring states' (Interview with the author).

---

[19] 'Gujarat Plagued by Vigilantes', *The Hindu*, 22 July 2016.
[20] 'Who is a Gau Rakshak', *Live Mint*, 26 July 2016.

It is in these states that most incidents of lynching have been reported.

> I can say with authority, nowhere do our volunteers kill people. They are cow lovers, they are not killers of human beings. They mostly nab the cow smugglers, and hand them over to the police. And they take the injured cattle to a vet or a gaushala. (Interview with the author)

How come then most killings are in this region? Take for instance, the cases from the lynching of Akhlaq in September 2015 to Rakbar in July 2018. 'I can say with certainty not one of our volunteers was involved in all these cases. Like in Rakbar, if his family was keeping cows as pets or for milk, why would our volunteers go and kill him?' (Interview with the author)

But it is often said, that the moment *gau rakshaks* see a Muslim man with cows, they pounce upon him....

> See, so many times, people kill to defame us. It could be local enmity. Or some local goons. Or even people affiliated with political parties like the Congress or the BJP. At times, even police beat up people they believe to be cow smugglers. But because of people's perception, our image suffers. (Interview with the author)

But whenever there is a lynching incident, some *gau rakshaks* are seen in videos killing the man, like it was with Qasim in Hapur, Akhlaq in Dadri or Rakbar in Alwar.

> We do not release such videos. I can say with guarantee our men did not kill Qasim or others. They are totally

non-violent. They do not carry any weapons. There have been cases like in Gurgaon when cow smugglers have fired at them, but they could not fire in self-defense because they had no arms with them. Our volunteers were fired at in Gurgaon on 25 Aug, 2016. In Himachal Pradesh too the volunteers were fired at. The families of the injured get affected too, but where can we talk of this? The problem is we never get a chance to clear the air. Even on television, people who come as cow experts, they would never have had a cow at home. They cannot distinguish one cow from another. They know nothing of cow breeds, yet they are called experts. Television has its own compulsions. They call one representative from the RSS, another from the BJP, somebody else from Congress or JDU. The real gau rakshaks who sacrifice their comfort and sleep are never there. (Interview with the author)

Having said that, Pandit reels out figures of their work.

It is not possible to count all the FIRs we file district-wise across the country. We are not sure of rescue numbers either but we do file seven to 10 FIRs every month. I am only counting the genuine one, not fake cases. Unlike what appears in media, we stand to gain nothing. Even the gaushalas we run operate on donations. (Interview with the author)

Incidentally, according to Pandit, over the past four years, since 2014, the number of cow shelters has gone up significantly.

Over the past five years, there are 5000 new gaushalas across the country. In Rajasthan, we have 2200 gaushalas operating. In Haryana, it is 1800. Most gaushalas can take up to 400 cattle, none more than 500. Some are so small that they can accommodate only 50 or 70 cows. We do get some support from the Government. That is usually not sufficient. We have to rely on voluntary donations. We put a box at a jeweller's shop or a drum at a public square to get some food and money for the cows. We send tempos too to the market. We get land from panchayats also as we tell them that stray cows wander into their fields at night and damage their crops. So it is better to keep them at a gaushala. It is the same with the bikers. We tell them that many accidents take place because of cows sitting in the middle of, or by the side of main roads. At night, it is difficult to see. So, it is best to set up gaushalas, leave the animals there in safety. But due to the media, the image is negative. People have wrong ideas about gau rakshaks. I agree some people may have done wrong, but they won't be from our BGRD. These days, so many people claim to be gau rakshaks. (Interview with the author)

He reveals that most *gau rakshaks* are Brahmins.

Some are Yadavas, Jats or Ahirs, but mostly only those can truly love the cow who have been doing it for generations, who have it in their blood. We do hear of Muslim gau rakshaks from the RSS Muslim Manch, but we say, they should not politicise the issue. (Interview with the author)

A Muslim becoming a cow protector is politics.

But is it not true that the police arrested a senior *gau rakshak* from Greater Noida for forcing meat shops to down their shutters? And Satish Kumar, the chief of Punjab Gau Raksha Dal was arrested for alleged sodomy, as some men from Saharanpur in Uttar Pradesh complained?

> Satish was arrested in Vrindavan. I concede some wrongs have taken place. I cannot deny that. There are so many types of people. It is like in politics now. This entire gau raksha movement has been made into a Hindu–Muslim issue for political benefits. But we must remember that even Gandhiji was against cow slaughter. He thought somebody who does that cannot be a Hindu. (Interview with the author)

But is it not true that *gau rakshaks* make it impossible for a Muslim to keep cows now? And that it is easy to lynch a Muslim man, grab his cows, then use them for your own economic benefit?

> This is wrong. We love cows, why would we kill for cows? And we do not bring rescued cattle home. They are given to the police to be sent to gaushalas. And if you are talking of the cattle, you must see their condition. Often they are in such a sad condition, one feels like crying. (Interview with the author)

Pandit then elaborates on the agrarian and scientific benefits of the cow.

> Cow is linked to faith but is also the cornerstone of rural economy. India is a predominantly agrarian, rural economy. At times of famine also, if one has a cow, it is sufficient to feed three-four family members. It is used for ploughing the field too. Forget religion, can we not ban cow slaughter everywhere for

economic reasons? We want every house to have a cow. If it is not possible to keep a cow, donate for a cow. Like they say in politics, Ghar ghar Modi, we say, Ghar ghar gaye. We are not anti-Muslim or anti-Dalit. We are a cow fraternity out to save our mother. Since we set out our organisation in 2012 we must have saved the lives of more 13,000 cows. (Interview with the author)

In an interview, he claimed, 'My workers call me when they come to know about any such (cow slaughter) incident. I immediately call the police; and in most if not every case, the police have supported us and accompanied us'.[21]

Today, he asks,

We are not against any religion or community. We are shanti priya (peace-lovers) by nature. We consume only the food provided by the Mother Earth. But do you know who eats beef? A person who kills the cow with one stroke, then hangs the body upside down cannot be a lover of peace. (Interview with the author)

But isn't this way of killing an animal practised by the Sikh community? The Muslims go for Halal which involves a slow cutting of the jugular vein. 'Whatever. See any community which eats beef. They practice violence. Not just here in India but across the world'.

His words are but a reiteration of what a Vishva Hindu Parishad member said in the defence of gau rakshaks. 'They are cow protectors. They are not killers. They cannot kill any human

---

[21] 'Who is a Gau Rakshak', *Live Mint*, 26 July 2016.

being'. And the vicious circle of cow protectors–cow killers continues to take many innocent lives. Just as it did in 1893 when communal riots in the name of the cow claimed more than a 100 victims. Or, 1966 when at least eight people paid with their life seeking a ban on cow slaughter. Or, even in 1979 when Vinoba Bhave sat on a hunger strike demanding a ban on cow slaughter. The modern-day *gau raksha dals* are merely continuing the sorry tradition of violence related to the cow. Incidentally, contrary to what Pandit would have had us believe, the largest beef-consuming state in India is not the Muslim-dominated Jammu and Kashmir or the Lakshawdweep islands, but Meghalaya, where more than 80 per cent people consume beef. No plans are afoot to appoint new *gau raksha dal* activists there.

Mind of a *Gau Rakshak*: All Hate, No Love?

All the men murdered in the name of *gau raksha* met with a merciless end. Some were left with their arms and legs bruised and bleeding. Almost all endured multiple fractures. Most had ribs broken. One man had his eye reduced to a socket. Another victim had one of his ears chopped off. One man's body reached his family in a mutilated condition, betraying prolonged torture. One man even had his nails pulled out. Nobody had a peaceful, or relatively peaceful, end. Their attackers were untouched by humanity. Driven by rage, they unleashed unceasing cruelty. Pray, what drives a man to inflict such barbarity in modern age? It cannot be for the love of Hinduism, an all-acquiescing faith that can assimilate more streams of thought than many an ocean. Nor can it realistically be for the love of the cow. A cow never kills. A cow lover should not kill. And this unrepentant streak of violence could not have been approved by Mahatma

File 1: Lynching

Gandhi, often quoted by *gau rakshaks* in their defence, for his love of the cow. As seasoned sociologist Professor Avijit Pathak said,

> In a way, violence is the negation of love; violence emanates from the broken communication; violence is related to selfish desire that reduces others to objects of use; violence emanates from narcissism, insecurity and a sense of meaninglessness. Lynching or mob violence is also a manifestation of this ugly culture. (Interview with the author)

So what makes a so-called *gau rakshak* a blood-thirsty monster?

In a society like ours—troubled over population explosion, scarcity of resources, limited job opportunities, widening gap between the rich and the poor, and hopelessness emanating from all-pervading corruption—people tend to feel a sense of existential void and powerlessness. This anonymity or absence of creative agency in life is more acute when you migrate, lose your organic or cultural roots, live as nameless masses. The result is anger. Not to forget a lingering feeling of anomie, a deep-seated alienation. In the absence of socio-economic cushion, this can manifest itself in the most bizarre or bloodiest of ways. Add to this feeling of normlessness, a peculiar Saraswati Shishu Mandir-kind of education system which probably tells them from the beginning that all Muslims were invaders; all are wife-beaters; all are beefeaters. They are brought up on skewed notions of 'we' and 'they'. In a couple of lynching incidents in the Alwar region, the cow vigilantes were desperate to lay hands at men before they crossed over to the Muslim-dominated part of Mewat region. In the case of Rakbar, a cow vigilante frankly expressed,

'We had to do something quickly. Ours is the last village before he (the alleged cow smuggler/victim) could cross over to his village. That is a Muslim village. They slaughter cows every day'. In the mind of a *gau rakshak*, every Muslim is a cow killer! Or, take the case of Alimuddin who was killed not in his Muslim-dominated village, but in town square with its cover of anonymity.

This deep prejudice and division of the world into 'we' and 'they' is accentuated by the cow militia's received and perceived notions of the sacredness of the cow. And it is not difficult to understand their aversion, even hostility towards the community. Worse, in the absence of a first person interaction with members of the community, these prejudices get deep seated.

> In an interview with *NewsClick*, some self-appointed *gau rakshaks* expressed their animosity towards Muslims thus: 'All our 33 crore deities abide in the stomach of the cow. And these people (Muslims) want to kill the cow. We won't let anybody kill the cow. She is our mother, the world's mother'.

A young man in his 20s, he had never heard of the families of Pehlu Khan or Rakbar who kept milch cows at home for generations. He had not heard of Professor D. N. Jha and his claims about the cow meat being served to deities in ancient India, either. He had lived in his bubble where space for reason, dialogue was absent, as was the ability to negotiate with the perceived 'other'. The windows of his mind, the doors of his life were all shut.

This anger, this hostility manifests itself every day in cases of road rage in urban India. An inability to start your vehicle with split second accuracy when the traffic signal turns green at an intersection invites stare and abuses. Parking the car a few feet from the designated slot attracts snarls. Nobody ever has time or patience to talk to the man next door. In such an atmosphere, a so-called *gau rakshak* lives in a virtual social vacuum. In his bubble, his prejudices grow, his anger stays simmering. Our psychologists might advise people to talk to each other, not talk at each other, but in the world of *gau rakshaks* all that is visible is the shadow of the self. There is just one way of being. Anybody who is different is an enemy. That is why, the *gau rakshaks* attack only the Muslims ferrying cows, not Hindus. For instance, in the case of Pehlu Khan, his Hindu driver was let off with just a slap and an admonition by cow militia. What happened to Pehlu and rest of the Muslim travellers needs no reiteration. The same thing happened in Chittorgarh where Hindu travellers with cattle were let off, the Muslims were thrashed, stripped and humiliated. Considering most *gau rakshaks* are at the lower steps of upward mobility when it comes to the economy, a chance to handle alleged cow smugglers comes as a God-sent. Suddenly, there is a vent for anger, an approbation of faith and maybe a chance to augment financial avenues. Also, often the cow militia is said to work in complicity with police, with the latter seen as passive bystander to their violent streak. This tacit approval of the state's official safety guard gives *gau rakshaks* a sense of invincibility.

However, there comes a little sad note. In the absence of a vibrant alternative/emancipatory political culture—and this is the tragedy of our times—this anger is misplaced. It is in this sense that communalism is a false consciousness. A poor Brahmin, a landless Sikh, a Muslim peasant do not come together, and strive for collective justice. Instead, the dominant ideology, often expressed in material terms, transforms them into antagonistic groups. Each act of lynching reproduces this distorted vision, helps the powerful to retain their rule and transforms the 'other-directed' crowd (directed by the propaganda machinery, the rumours and the constant hate campaign) into a mindless mob without clarity, reflexivity, political maturity, conscience and educational sensibilities. Cow vigilantism, killing people in the name of 'child lifters', and even physically abusing a leader like Swami Agnivesh, who too was attacked in Jharkhand—reveals the absence of reason, shared humanism and the intensity of aggression that has entered the psyche of people in a violent society with its characteristic alienation and depression. It seems that to kill the projected 'enemy' is the only way to find one's 'agency' in this dehumanized world!

'"Inna lillahi wa inna ilayhi raji'un—From Allah we come, and to Allah we shall return." The Muslims recite this verse from the Quran at the time of someone's death. I recite this not because Akhlaq, Pehlu and Qasim are dead but because it is humanity which is dead'. These words of Sana Khan, a PhD scholar from Jawaharlal Nehru University, ring in one's ears, as one tries to make sense of the actions of a *gau rakshak*.

Indeed, with each new incident, we plummet further to new levels of human degradation. The real danger lies not in the strength of the bad/evil, but in the weakness of good. As Khan says,

> I ask myself, I am having dinner with my family, and suddenly fifty or hundred people enter my house,

and start beating us, what would I do? How would I respond? Death would seem to come closer. We live in a society which has become extremely intolerant; has lost all moral sense, of life, of home, of tradition, of integrated communities—and we are placed in the midst of a depraved universe. (Interview with the author)

Clearly, the mind of a *gau rakshak* has little space for love, none for debate or dissent. It is not even about the cow. It is only about hatred of the 'other'.

File 2

Muslims: Easy Targets?

OMEN OF THINGS TO COME

As 45-year-old Jaan Mohammed lifted the sheet of cloth, face downwards, from the body of his brother, he was horrified. Fifty-two-year-old Akhlaq was not just murdered by neighbourhood cow militia but bruised, battered and brutalized to death. His neighbours did to him
what a wolf does to half-eaten deer in the jungle. One of Akhlaq's ears was completely chopped, the other half lobbed off; one of his lips was slit, the other swollen stiff. He still bled from his nose, his face. His right eye was soaked in blood. His skin from the cheekbone to chin was peeled off from one side of the face. His skull was fractured. His fractured left arm just hung in there. The nape of his neck was broken. As were his ribs, his wrists and ankles. Knees fractured, his legs just hung like a piece of clothing from a hanger. There were marks of lynching, peeling of skin, slitting of flesh on his body, from torso to toes. 'There was not a part of his body left intact', recalls his brother Jaan Mohammed nearly three years after Akhlaq met with a gory end. The passage of time did little to heal the wounds. Even today, the abuses of his attackers,

including a man in a checked shirt, another in saffron shorts, yet another in a vest and drawers as they surrounded Akhlaq, as he breathed his last, ring in his mind. The video spread online. It reached Akhlaq's sons too. And depending on where you stood on the side of the word spread: A cow killer was done to death by *gau rakshaks* in Dadri. Or, an innocent man lynched by cow terrorists?

On that day, however, as Jaan Mohammed mustered up courage to give his brother a ceremonial ghusl (bath) before the *namaz-e-janaaza* (funeral prayer), both Jaan Mohammed and his brother went into a shiver. Their hands trembled as they tried to clean the badly bruised and bleeding body of their brother. Somehow, the ghusl with lukewarm water in which the leaves of a neem tree were sprinkled was done, but it was not easy. Splashing a tumbler of water over the right shoulder, then the left was a painful exercise. The body, laid on a wooden plank for bathing, creaked as the male family members sought to move from one side to the other for cleaning. From head to toe, somehow, the body was cleaned, gently, lovingly, painfully. Along the way, tears of his brothers got mixed with the tumblers of water. Then the body was wrapped in a white shroud. This again was difficult, as there was little to hold the body together due to multiple fractures. If the mourners put their arm under the head, they discovered a hollow. If they put their arms around the waist, they could sense a broken bone. And some marks of blood just refused to be washed away, defiant to enter the grave with the body in whose veins it ran until a few hours earlier.

AKHLAQ

As Akhlaq's brothers and son set out with the *janaaza* (funeral procession), the wails at home were muffled, weeping persistent. The women controlled their tears by covering their faces with dupattas, the men preferred to look at the ground, too shy to be seen with tears in their eyes. Akhlaq's daughter Shaista let out the loudest cry.

> No neighbour stepped forward to lend a shoulder to the *janaaza*; many of whom had, for years, joined Akhlaq and his family over Eid-ul-Azha celebrations, and relished the special biryani and sewaiyan made on the occasion. Not everybody was communal.

Not everybody believed Akhlaq had killed a calf. All had been silenced and distanced by the aggressive cow militia which had claimed in Akhlaq its first major victim. Akhlaq's sorry end was to embolden the alleged cow terrorists to spread their network far and wide, striking at a moment when the 'enemy' would be most vulnerable: either in anticipation of Eid or exulting after one; the effect too would be devastating. Akhlaq too was massacred hours after Eid-ul-Azha celebrations.

A couple of Muslim neighbours, and some relatives managed to make it for the funeral. Not everybody could. Among them were Akhlaq's nephews and nieces who were denied permission by the police, citing prohibitory orders. The imam of the local masjid of Bishara, Akhlaq's ancestral village, led the prayers before he was laid to rest at the age-old *qabrastan* (cemetery) of the village. As Akhlaq was lowered

File 2: Muslims: Easy Targets?

into the grave, a brother of Akhlaq stepped in to receive the wobbly body with gentle, soft hands. Then, as he lay the body on the somewhat dry soil, he turned Akhlaq's face towards *qibla* (prayer direction). After all the injuries and insult, he could complain to God and seek justice.

Just a little later, Mahesh Sharma, a local member of parliament (MP), and also a union minister, came to Akhlaq's residence. In a widely televised brief appearance, not exceeding three minutes, he advised the family to 'forget it (Akhlaq's killing) as an accident'. 'It was an accident. Not pre-planned. That's all'. The words were very much in consonance with the argument taken around three years later when, in June 2018, two of the men accused of Akhlaq's murder, approached Jaan Mohammed to withdraw the case against them as it was merely an accident, and promised to do the same themselves. Incidentally, a year after Akhlaq's departure, a case was foisted on the family of Akhlaq, accusing them of cow slaughter. And Jaan Mohammed was made the principal accused. Jaan Mohammed declined the offer of truce, promising to fight for justice for his brother.

It is a fight that will take a lot of time and could come with several emotional challenges. Like, for instance, the day Mahesh Sharma showed up again in his village. This time he spent more than a couple of hours to share the grief of the family members of Ravin Sisodia, one of the men accused of killing Akhlaq. Sisodia had died in prison, allegedly of dengue. The family believed otherwise and for three days refused to cremate the body. There were allegations of a deadly quarrel among the prisoners inside the prison. And Sharma stepped in to wipe their tears, and send Sisodia for his last journey wrapped like a brave soldier of the nation in our national flag.

> Killing a Muslim after accusing him of cow slaughter seemed a new duty in the age of rampant majoritarianism. Deed done, the national flag was there to be wrapped around the alleged murderer. That is how murder accused Sisodia departed from this world.

Battered, broken, bleeding; that is how Akhlaq, the father of a serving Indian Air Force personnel, started his final journey. Amazingly, Akhlaq's son Mohammed Sartaj when asked to give a message in those troubled times, said, '*Sare jahan se achcha Hindustan hamara*'. And, as Jaan Mohammed revealed, the family buried Akhlaq without any protest. The body was not laid on the town square to draw public attention. No compensation was demanded. Not even a demand for the arrest of the accused. Just a quiet private final journey of a man who had lived in Dadri's Bishara village for long years.

Sharma was not the only political figure from the ruling dispensation to lend overt or covert support to Akhlaq's murderers. Former BJP MLA Nawab Singh Nagar blamed the victim's family, saying, 'If they have consumed beef, they are also responsible. This is a village of Thakurs and they express their sentiments in a very strong way. If they have done this, they should have kept in mind what the reaction would be'. 'Whose blood won't boil if they see cow slaughter?' echoed Shrichand Sharma, Vice President of BJP's western Uttar Pradesh unit. Sharma, not to be left behind, indicated that Akhlaq's 17-year-old daughter should be grateful she wasn't raped! And the fact that she was not assaulted meant the murderers of her father were hurt by cow slaughter, and were not men of low integrity.

Less than 20 days after Akhlaq's gory end, his family, and those of his brothers, left their village. Initially, the family shifted to Chennai where Akhlaq's son Sartaj was posted. Then, as Sartaj was transferred to Delhi on his request, the family left Dadri for good. Akhlaq's brothers are no longer together. The eldest brother Jameel stays in Loni now, two others, Jaan and Akhtiar, stay in Dadri. Earlier, the four brothers lived on the same plot of land, their nuclear families mixing with joint family members all the time.

Each one of them awaits justice for their slain brother, desperate to get the accusation of cow killing wiped off their slate.

> Nobody in our khandaan (family) has ever eaten cow meat. I remember five generations here, you can ask any villager if we have had even a quarrel with a neighbour. Never. We have been here for 70 years. Two days after the murder, our neighbours started approaching me for rapprochement as I am better educated. We were not ready for negotiation. Why should we agree for a truce when my brother was innocent? We were asked to take back Akhlaq's murder case. If we are with truth, we will win. There were some 18 or 19 accused, their guardians, relatives and family members who came down. But I repeated that it was not an accident. It was a planned murder. They made an announcement from Shiv Mandir here. The pujari asked people to gather near a transformer, which is a 100 metres or so from Akhlaq's residence. People gathered there, and planned. It was around 9 pm or so when they attacked Akhlaq. He had just finished his dinner

Lynch Files

after Isha prayers, and retired to his bedroom. (Jaan Mohammed, in an interview with the author)

So, how did it all devolve down to a gruesome lynching of a man sleeping at his home in the privacy of his bedroom? Well, in the evening of the fatal day, a calf had reportedly gone missing. And some neighbours accused Akhlaq of stealing and slaughtering the animal. Akhlaq denied the allegation. The neighbours refused to believe that he had not killed the calf as part of Eid celebrations. An announcement was allegedly made from the temple where Akhlaq was pronounced guilty of killing the calf. A crowd gathered at the transformer and then marched to Akhlaq's house, carrying sticks and bricks. The mob attacked the house, raided the fridge, dragged Akhlaq and his son Danish who were sleeping, outside to the road where the two of them were repeatedly hit with sticks and bricks. Danish suffered serious injuries and had to be treated at Kailash Hospital in Noida where he had to undergo a brain surgery, then another. Akhlaq succumbed to his injuries. The police arrested the temple priest soon after besides 10 of the accused, based on the testimony of Akhlaq's family. Among them was Vishal, son of local BJP leader Sanjay Rana. The priest denied his involvement in the issue, arguing that he was forced to make the announcement by some local youngsters. He also denied naming Akhlaq in the announcement.

'The police only put the names given by our family members in the list of the accused. Nobody else was nabbed', says Jaan Mohammed. Among the men arrested, some were out on bail after some time. They were rehabilitated with temporary jobs at a thermal power corporation besides an automobile giant in the area. Two of them work in the same office as Jaan Mohammed.

Akhlaq's mother, widow, sons and brothers all wait for justice. The then Chief Minister of Uttar Pradesh Akhilesh Yadav gave a compensation of ₹5 lakh each to the brothers, and ₹30 lakh to the widow of Akhlaq. The central government under Prime Minister Narendra Modi did not give any compensation to the family of the killed. Jaan Mohammed moans,

> The Prime Minister did not even speak a word of sympathy. Not even the routine sentences like assuring us that the accused will be nabbed, etc. He spoke about Rohit Vemula, yes. He spoke about Dalit lynching saying, kill me before killing a Dalit. But he did not say a word of sympathy to us or express any regret.[22]

There are a few questions though for which the family seeks answers. There have been contradictory reports of forensic science laboratories about the meat. While initially, a local laboratory declared that the meat seized from Akhlaq's fridge was mutton, not beef, later another laboratory reversed the findings. Asks Jaan Mohammed,

> The police in their charge-sheet which they submitted to the court after 88 days, said, 'We took Akhlaq from the road for hospitalisation. We took Danish from home.' How did they get one person from the house, the other from the road? According to the police, they came to the house around 10:30 p.m. and took meat from the fridge around 1:00 a.m. In the intervening period, anybody could have put anything in the fridge in the melees that was going on. First of all, the police had no right to open our private fridge. When I reached Akhlaq's home around 5:00 a.m., I found police in

---

[22] 'Dalit Suicide Case: Why Rohith Vemula's Death is the Tipping Point in Caste Bias on Campus', available at: //economictimes.indiatimes.com/articleshow/50698749.cms?utm_source=contentofinterest&utm_medium=text&utm_campaign=cppst

 Lynch Files

every nook and corner of the house. My aged mother was hiding in a bathroom. Police got hold of rods with names like Rana and Thakur written on them. There was an iron rod, plenty of bricks used to hit him too. The police was still there. They should have got evidence from our house if there was any of cow slaughter. They did not. (Jaan Mohammed, in an interview with the author)

Instead, he says,

> The police put the meat recovered from the fridge in plastic bags and sent it to Pashu Chikatsalaya in Dadri. The police never clarified which officer or constable took the meat. Anyway, the Pashu Chikatsalaya said it had examined the meat, and from the legs, skin of the face, four to five inches of meat, it concluded it was mutton, red in colour. However, when the police took the meat from our home, it was entered as 2.5 kg. But later, it was said to be 4.5 kg. From where did the extra meat come? If the police had any suspicion of cow slaughter, why did they not send the leg pieces of the animal to a forensic laboratory? Anybody can say after looking at the legs if the animal was a cow or a goat. Then, after second investigation, even Central Forensic and Scientific Laboratory in Mathura declared that the meat was mutton. *Amar Ujala*, dated 30 December 2015, made it a headline that the laboratory had corroborated the Dadri laboratory findings. It validated the family's contention that Akhlaq had been killed by right-wing people on a fake charge. Yet, after some time, the same meat was pronounced to be beef! From the beginning, there has been too much politics in the case. The powers that be do not want to arrive at the truth. They know it was not beef,

FIGHTING ONE MORE ROUND: Akhlaq's brother, Jaan Mohammed (in black), and his son Sartaj fighting a legal battle to prove his innocence.

and they will go to any extent to say it was. Also, let me recall that when the police initially arrested five men for the murder, they confessed, saying they were instigated into doing that by some local boys. They said they could recognize those boys. But the police never brought them face to face with the people who allegedly instigated them into killing my brother. (Jaan Mohammed, in an interview with the author)

The fight goes on. Meanwhile, Greater Noida Developmental Authority handed over four flats to the kin of Akhlaq. Among the four flats, one was registered in the name of Akhlaq's widow, Ikraman, whereas, three others were in the names of his brothers. And Sadhvi Harshita Giri who took over as the new priest of the village temple announced a *shuddhikaran* (purification) ceremony in Dadri. It has been around three years since the first lynching instance of our times hit the headlines. There is no abating the crime, and Akhlaq's brothers continue to live a life of insecurity and fear.

> Insecurity is there all the time. On Eid too one just wishes for a peaceful passage of time. I won't say every neighbour is in the wrong. Just as all human

beings cannot be wrong, the entire village cannot do something wrong. It is only because of a handful of people that we have suffered. Akhlaq will not come back. His body was badly hurt, but his soul should rest content that justice will be done to him, and his name will be cleaned of the stigma of cow slaughter. (Jaan Mohammed, in an interview with the author)

A relatively young body, Hindu Rashtra Sena (HRS), is quickly making up for its late entry in the politics of hate and harvest. It first caught attention when its chief Dhananjay Desai shared the stage with well-known Hindutva proponent, Shri Ram Sene Pramod Muthalik's and Abhinav Bharat's Himani Savarkar.

Desai though had earned his spurs. By the time he was invited to address the Hindu Rashtra Convention in Goa in 2013, he faced 23 cases of extortion, riots and other crimes. Yet the body really hit the headlines when 24-year-old IT professional Mohsin Shaikh was lynched allegedly by 21 members of HRS in Pune. Shaikh was coming back after offering Isha prayers around 9:00 PM and picking up dinner at a takeaway. He was with his friend Riyaz when the members of the radical Hindu outfit attacked him.

According to Riyaz, Shaikh was attacked near his rented flat in Bankar Colony in Hadaspur.

File 2: Muslims: Easy Targets?

> He was made the target allegedly because he looked like a typical Muslim, with a skullcap and a beard. Shaikh was assaulted by a mob of over 20 people, with hockey sticks, bats and stones, leading to his death.

Although the police soon called Desai for questioning, and arrested the seven accused, Shaikh paid with his life. He was declared brought dead when taken to a private hospital around 1:00 AM.

It was the first instance of lynching after the BJP-led government was sworn in at the Centre. It set caution notes ringing, considering the dastardly act took place in just about a week of the change in dispensation at the Centre. Many read in it as a bad omen. Indians, unused to American-style lynching based on race, were appalled at the barbarity of the act and wished for immediate punishment. Nobody though was yet ready to believe that it was to be the beginning of a series of lynchings over the next few years.

Most though were ready to wish it away as a one-off case where fringe elements of Hindutva had allowed themselves to be swayed by the heat of the moment. Modi's honeymoon with the nation had barely started and a large part of the society and polity was reluctant to sour the mood. Shaikh could as well be collateral damage in nation's renewed tryst with destiny. His family and friends mourned the passing away of the talented techie, which happened because of some morphed photographs of Shivaji and Bal Thackeray that he had allegedly put on his Facebook wall.

Yet even the detractors of the Hindutva movement believed that Shaikh will be given justice at least in death. After all, he

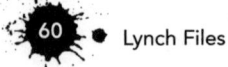

had provoked no one. He kept no cow, did not slaughter one either. Nor did he insult any Maratha icon. He was a suave, urban technocrat for whom difference in religion meant an opportunity to debate or to have a dialogue. By no stretch of imagination could he be dubbed a cow killer or a Shivaji hater. He had a far better grooming, and too much at stake to really bother about people's rituals. Yet, lynched he was!

The worse was to come a little later. As the nation waited for exemplary punishment for the guilty, Ujwal Nikam took over as the public prosecutor for the aggrieved party. Shaikh's family was relieved as Nikam enjoyed their faith, having successfully pleaded the 26/11 case besides the Gulshan Kumar murder case. However, after two and a half years of litigation, in January 2017, Justice Mridula Bhatkar of Bombay High Court observed,

> The fault of the deceased was only that he belonged to another religion. I consider this factor in favour of the applicants/accused. Moreover, the applicants/accused do not have any criminal record and it appears that in the name of the religion, they were provoked and have committed the murder.[23]

She granted bail to 3 of the 21 accused with her order. Bhatkar said,

> The meeting was held half an hour prior to the assault. The accused otherwise had not other motive such as any personal enmity against innocent deceased Mohsin. The fault of the deceased was only that he belonged to another religion. I consider this factor

---

[23] 'Violence in Name of Religion cannot be Justified: Supreme Court', available at: http://timesofindia.indiatimes.com/articleshow/62934313.cms?utm_source=contentofinterest&utm_medium=text&utm_campaign=cppst

File 2: Muslims: Easy Targets?

in favour of the applicants/accused. Moreover, the accused do not have criminal record and it appears that in the name of the religion, they were provoked and have committed the murder.[24]

Six months later, to the disappointment of the family, Nikam quit the case.

It was the first time one heard of difference in faith as being reason enough to be killed. The fact that the deceased followed another religion went in favour of the accused who were provoked in the name of religion and seem to have committed the murder!

A little more than a year later, in February 2018, the Supreme Court quashed the bail of the three accused. The three accused—Vijay Rajendra Gambhire, Ganesh alias Ranjeet Shankar Yadav and Ajay Dilip Lalge—were among the 21 HRS activists, including their leader Dhananjay Desai alias Bhai, who were booked in connection with the murder of Shaikh in Hadapsar on 2 June 2014. The Supreme Court bench of Justices S. A. Bobde and Nageshwar Rao remanded the matter back for fresh hearing after holding that the reasons cited by the High Court were 'vulnerable to criticism' even though the High Court judge may not have intended to hurt the feelings of any particular community or support the feelings of another. The Supreme Court bench observed that the High Court order showed little discussion on the merit of the case. The 'reason given by the HC can be understood or misunderstood ... as a kind of justification for the murder and it is obvious that the fact deceased belonged to

---

[24] 'Cannot Justify Murder saying Victim belonged to a "certain community": SC', available at: https://www.thehindu.com/news/national/cannot-justify-murder-saying-victim-belonged-to-a-certain-community-sc/article22759193.ece

Lynch Files

a certain community cannot be a justification for any assault much less a murder'.

There was more solace to come for Shaikh's family. More than four years after he was beaten to death, his family received compensation from the Maharashtra government. Through a government resolution, the State Revenue Department announced a compensation of ₹5 lakh from the state fund and a matching amount from the central fund. The government resolution directed authorities at the Pune Collectorate to handover ₹10 lakh to Shaikh's family. This came in response to Shaikh's father, Sadiq, approaching the Human Rights Law Network in July 2017 for adequate compensation for the death of his son. 'The HRLN had filed a writ petition in the Bombay High Court. I believe this has prompted the State government to finally act and provide us compensation', *The Hindu* quoted Mr Sadiq Shaikh.[25] The family though has still not been provided a job for the younger son, Mobin. And the promised compensation from the Centre is yet to fructify too, leaving the Shaikh family with only a compensation of ₹5 lakh for the murder of their sole earning member. The fight goes on in the first lynching case to hit the headlines since Narendra Modi Government assumed the reins of power in May 2014. Sadiq is not giving up yet. In an interview with *The Wire*, he said,

> When Mohsin was murdered, the administration was under severe pressure but my family and I never let the situation spiral into a riot. The tension was such that people on both sides were ready to kill each other. I can never forgive them for what they did to my son, but the right to punish lies with the judiciary.[26]

---

[25] 'Mohsin Shaikh's Kin get Compensation', *The Hindu*, 16 June 2018.
[26] 'Even After Nikam's Withdrawal From Case, Mohsin Shaikh's Family Has Not Lost Hope for Justice', *The Wire*, available at: https://thewire.in/law/nikam-withdrawal-from-case-mohsin-shaikh-family-not-lost0jope-for-justice.

THE *GAU RAKSHAKS* OF RAJASTHAN

'My father was killed because he had a beard'. These words of Pehlu Khan's 24-year-old son Irshad said it all. He was speaking nearly three weeks after his father, 55-year-old Pehlu Khan, was brutally assaulted and killed by cow vigilantes when he was coming home after purchasing some animals from a cattle fair. Pehlu was killed not because he was going to slaughter the cows—he was a dairy farmer and not a butcher—but because he was a Muslim. His murder deprived Irshad and his younger brother Arif of their father. It tore apart the peace of Mewat too as Pehlu was a Meo. His village Jaisinghpur in Haryana's Nuh tehsil is dominated by Meo Muslims, although there is a significant number of Hindu households too. The two communities stayed in peace and harmony. That was until the *gau rakshaks* spoiled it all.

Alwar Lynchings
PEHLU KHAN
April 2017

On 1 April 2017, some men on bikes thrashed Pehlu Khan, who was returning home from a cattle fair in Jaipur. Pehlu and his two sons had purchased two milch cows and as many calves for ₹45,000. Two of their fellow villagers too purchased milch cattle from the fair. Keeping in mind the troubled times ever since Akhlaq was murdered, they procured receipts for the animals for good measure. It did not prove good enough.

At around 7:00 PM, some cow vigilantes intercepted the vehicle in which Pehlu was travelling with Azmat, a fellow villager. They were on the Delhi–Jaipur highway in Rajasthan's Alwar district, and not too far from home.

They were pulled out and beaten with belts and hockey sticks while a sizable crowd watched before some members of the crowd too joined in. As Pehlu first tried to prove his innocence, then pleaded for his and his companion's life, he was felled to the ground, with men now taking turns to hit and kick him. The attackers tore the clothes of the victims, who had later to be provided some clothes by the police to keep their dignity. The attackers went away with the cash that Pehlu and the others possessed, besides their mobile phones and watches. Even the cows. They planned to set them on fire but for the arrival of the police. A video was made of the assault and soon uploaded online.

Soon, the other vehicle carrying milch cattle, with Pehlu's sons and a villager, followed. Once again, the men were dragged out of the vehicle and thrashed in full public view. Nobody stepped forward to help. Pehlu though was the worst sufferer. The boys were both clean-shaven, as were the two village men. Pehlu had a distinctly Muslim beard with a trimmed upper lip. He suffered the most.

An FIR was registered on the basis of Pehlu's complaint wherein he mentioned that the attackers identified themselves as activists of the Vishva Hindu Parishad and Bajrang Dal. They told him that whoever transported cattle on the Behror route would meet the same fate. The FIR named six persons

File 2: Muslims: Easy Targets?

and said that the assailants included 200 other unidentified persons. However, none of them was apprehended.

Shockingly, in the wake of the murder, Rajasthan Police filed a case against Pehlu under the Rajasthan Bovine Animals (Prohibition of Slaughter and Regulation of Temporary Migration or Export) Act, 1995. Eleven farmers from Mewat were booked under the Bovine Act under sections relating to inter-state transportation of cattle. It was claimed that they did not have valid documents for inter-state travel, even as Pehlu's sons revealed that they had shown the cow purchase documents at various check posts before presenting the same to vigilantes as proof of their innocence. The so-called *gau rakshaks* tore the receipts apart.

Later, a delegation of Communist Party of India (Marxist) leaders met the deputy superintendent of police, district magistrate and other high officials, and discovered that the Jaipur Municipal Corporation had levied extra charges for inter-state transport of cattle. The delegation asked for an investigation into illegal checkpoints or 'Hindu *chowkis*' established by cow vigilantes. They were also told that the transporters did not have valid documents for inter-state travel. It was an allegation countered both by Pehlu's family and by the leaders of the delegation.

'If what we were doing was illegal, the Rajasthan Police would have stopped us. We had milch cows. No one kills milch cows. We are dairy farmers. We sell milk for a living', Arif explained. He further added, 'As Eid was approaching, and our buffalo was not giving a good yield, we had to buy milch cattle. Milch cows are cheaper than buffaloes'.

'If it was illegal, then why did the Jaipur municipality allow the sale', asked Hannan Mollah of the Kisan Sabha. He later played an active role in providing relief to the affected families. Additionally, with the official relief nowhere to be seen, Mollah and other political leaders were aided by the New Delhi-based Jamaat-e-Islami which got Pehlu's sons treated in Delhi even as financial relief was provided to the family to tide over the crisis, as their cows too were impounded in the attack.

In September 2017, the state police decided against pressing charges against the accused who were named by Pehlu from his hospital bed in his dying declaration. The state's Criminal Investigation Department said its investigations showed that the six accused were not involved in the attack. Hence, their names were struck off the FIR. It was claimed that the decision had been reached following examination of the evidence, including photographs of the crime scene and the location of the six men based on their cellular data.

The police refuted too the contention that the violence was planned, opting instead to treat it as a spontaneous outpouring. Hence, it filed a closure report, much to the dismay of Pehlu's family. The family, facing steep odds, pledged to fight back. Pehlu's son Irshad asked, 'Those six men named by our father stopped our vehicles. They mobilized the mob and started the assault. How could they not be guilty?'

Indeed!

So, who killed Pehlu? Not the men named by Pehlu—Om Yadav, Hukum Chand, Sudhir Yadav, Naveen Sharma, Rahul Saini and Jagmal Yadav. His statement being,

> About 200 men stopped our vehicle and started abusing and assaulting us. While assaulting, they were taking the names of Om Yadav, Hukum Chand, Naveen Sharma, Sudheer, Rahul Saini and Jagmal between

them, and saying that they are members of the Vishva Hindu Parishad and Bajrang Dal. They said whoever passes through Behror with cows will be beaten up like this.[27]

The six men, as reported by *The Indian Express*, were wanted by the Rajasthan police on various charges, including murder.[28] Five months later, police found them not guilty following an investigation during which the men, declared absconding, could not be questioned.

The Indian Express report stated,

> The six he named were initially wanted under IPC Sections 143 (unlawful assembly), 323 (voluntarily causing hurt), 341 (wrongful restraint), 306 (culpable homicide), 379 (theft) and 427 (destruction of property). Following Pehlu's death, 302 (murder) was added. Having found them not guilty, the police have withdrawn the reward of Rs. 5000 they had announced on each of the six men.[29]

Instead, nine other men will be tried for his murder. Seven of these men were identified from the video uploaded online. The other two were added to the case based on investigation. Three of them, Ravindra, Vipin and Kalu Ram, were granted bail by the Rajasthan High Court. Pehlu's family, meanwhile, is not ready to believe that the names Pehlu gave in his last statement to police were wrong, and is gearing up to fight all the way to the Supreme Court to get the guilty convicted.

---

[27] 'How a Botched Investigation Helped Get Six Accused in Pehlu Khan's Killing off the Hook', available at: https://thewire.in/rights/pehlu-khan-alwar-lynching-rajasthan-police-investigation
[28] 'Named in Dying Statement, Not Questioned, and "Not Guilty"', *The Indian Express*, 15 September 2017.
[29] Ibid.

Meanwhile, among those injured, Azmat still struggles to walk. He just wants to be on his feet like in the days prior to the assault. 'We are dairy farmers. Which dairy farmer kills his animal?' he asks from his charpoy.

'We will never go back to dairying', declares Rafiq, one of those injured in the attack.

Pehlu's sons struggle to make ends meet. Twenty-seven-year-old Irfan drives a truck. Mubarak, 22, drives a small tractor gifted by the Kisan Sabha, Irshad is the only one pursuing studies, courtesy Jamaat-e-Islami Hind which is footing the expenditure of his studies. And Pehlu's 80-year-old visually challenged mother just wants to hear her son's voice once more, as indeed do his eight children. There is collateral damage too.

> The biryani stalls, the kabab corners, the korma cauldrons have all disappeared from the region. They used buffalo meat in their preparations. Some tried to replace buffalo meat with chicken after state authorities decided to take samples from some dhabas. Others opted to shut down.

Today, nobody wants to take the risk for the fear of being branded a cow killer. Their main source of income gone, like Pehlu's family, they see an uncertain, insecure future.

If the idea behind attacking Pehlu and uploading the video was to instil fear in the community, it has worked. The bearded, the burqa-clad want to take no chances.

The Alwar attack may yet prove to be more damaging than initially thought. Meanwhile, a female cow vigilante called Vipin Yadav a modern-day Bhagat Singh!

Harsh Mander at the Site of Pehlu Khan's Lynching

The Police Stopping Harsh Mander from Paying Homage to the Departed

Rakbar Khan was a milkman whose earnings from the trade did not quite suffice to look after his family of two aged parents, a wife and seven little children, the youngest of whom was two, the oldest 12. So when a chance presented itself, he looked for avenues for additional income.
Every now and then, he would work as a daily wager at odd jobs. The earnings from that too were meagre. One day he decided to add to his bovine collection to supply more milk and make some more money for his children's education. As he had no funds, he borrowed some money from his mother-in-law, and a friend added a small amount from his side. Rakbar finally had ₹60,000 to buy two cows and calves for his shed. However, memories of Pehlu Khan's killing were fresh in everyone's mind. So Rakbar decided not to buy cattle during the daytime, but bring the animals home at night to avoid any trouble. For good measure, he took with him his friend of many years, Aslam.

Together, the two of them bought a couple of cows and calves. In the pitch darkness of Ramgarh in Alwar, not far from the border of Haryana, the two men walked the animals, kept securely on a leash. However, one cow strayed a little bit towards the green fields adjacent to the road. All hell broke loose. The villagers saw the two young men, and taking them to be cow thieves, attacked them with rods, hammers, axes, etc. In the melee, Aslam escaped to the forest nearby while Rakbar took the brunt of the villagers' anger.

The thrashing continued till Rakbar was almost unconscious. Then, around 12:45 AM. local police was informed by one Nawal Kishore, said to be a member of the Vishva Hindu Parishad.

File 2: Muslims: Easy Targets?

As the police took time in coming, Nawal Kishore drove down to the station himself to bring them to the site where Rakbar sat dazed, battered and bruised. Due to rain, the field was soggy. There were multiple footmarks, giving a clear indication of the involvement of more than a couple of persons. The police seized the animals, put Rakbar into their vehicle and drove off, first allegedly to the police station where they refreshed themselves with a cup of tea, then to a neighbouring Jain Gaushala where the animals were deposited. Then finally, at 4 AM, Rakbar was taken to a community health centre where the doctor pronounced him dead on arrival. He had died of internal bleeding due to heavy beating. Thus, a distance of about 4 kilometres from the spot of the attack to the hospital was covered in more than three hours by the police, a delay which proved fatal for Rakbar. Three men were arrested soon from Lalawandi village for attacking and murdering Rakbar Khan. Rakbar's family was informed of his demise at 7:00 AM through the village sarpanch.

Aslam was yet to resurface after the attack when, within hours of Akbar's murder, NDTV came up with a report wherein it was alleged,

> 'The man who died in Rajasthan's Alwar after being beaten by a mob on suspicion of cattle smuggling was in police custody for three hours before he was taken to a hospital early on Saturday'.

Lynch Files

It was alleged that 'the police arranged for vehicles to take the seized cows to a shelter, visited the police station—a stone's throw from the hospital—and even stopped for tea before getting medical help for the injured man. By the time they did, he was dead'.

An eyewitness, said to be Nawal Kishore's aunt, also told NDTV that she saw the police beating the injured man inside the vehicle. He was later allegedly given a wash and a fresh pair of clothes as he was 'too muddied'.

After the report was aired, the investigation was transferred to a senior officer of police. Assistant Sub-inspector Mohan Singh was suspended, while two constables, among them Harinder who was seen in a video kicking Rakbar inside the vehicle, were shifted to Police Lines as the police admitted to a delay in taking the injured to the hospital, although they termed as false and fabricated allegations of collusion in the victim's murder. 'We have no information yet about the victim being thrashed in custody, but yes, prima facie we have found that there was indeed an error in judgment in deciding what was important at that point', news agency ANI quoted NRK Reddy, special director general of police, as saying on the role of the police, a day after an NDTV investigation detected lapses on their part.

However, that was only one side of the Alwar coin. On the other side were allegations of a planned murder rather than a spontaneous attack by the villagers on seeing two men walk with the cow in the dark. There were allegations of the involvement of Nawal Kishore, who took a photograph of a dazed Rakbar sitting inside the police vehicle. Kishore posted the photo online to buttress his contention that the man died in police custody and was not lynched to death by cow vigilantes.

'See I took this picture in the police vehicle. He looks fine', Kishore said.

While the police negligence has been recorded, what cannot be denied in the whole sordid saga is that Rakbar was first lynched by cow vigilantes in Lalawandi village, close to Haryana. The villagers claimed that Muslim men had been passing through their fields at night on their way to Haryana. They would walk with cattle. So the villagers decided to seek the help of local *gau rakshaks* who lynched Rakbar and Aslam, although the latter managed to escape with his life. Thus, Rakbar was killed not on any proof but mere assumption of the villagers that he was a cow smuggler, and not a milkman, and that the cows were being transported to be butchered. Again, no proof was sought.

The police, in a classic demonstration of being one with the accused, called Rakbar 'a cow smuggler'. As reported by *The Wire*, the local farmers were convinced that the men were cattle smugglers.[30]

> It was the fourth time in the last 14 days that these men were taking the cows through this shortcut to their village. They would choose a time to cross our fields when there would be the least chance of anybody being present. For the past few days, we had noticed the footprints of men and cows in our fields but we could not dare to stop them single-handedly…. So we informed some local men who claimed to be working for gau raksha about this problem. Our farms are the last spot where these smugglers could be caught, Beyond these,

---

[30] 'Ground Report: "VHP Men the Main Culprits in Alwar Lynching, Police Role Secondary"', *The Wire*, 24 July 2018.

the Mohammedan area starts. There, [...] they openly sell beef and you cannot question anybody.[31]

So the so-called *gau rakshaks* lay in wait for Rakbar who had no clue what lay in store for him. Then they assaulted Rakbar and his friend. Rakbar was badly thrashed, his bones broken, his clothes muddied in the field in the monsoon season.

The police, while admitting to a lapse in taking the victim to the hospital, denied allegations of giving the victim a bath or a change of clothes to hide any wrongdoing. However, the medical report of the community health centre buttressed the contention when it said the victim was dry. Later, during a ceremonial bath before burial, Rakbar's family discovered the extent of his injuries. 'We saw that his legs, hands and neck bones were broken in three or four parts'. The autopsy report revealed broken ribs too. It had resulted in water entering his lungs.

A little later, a shaken Aslam appeared on the scene, guilt-ridden at having not been able to help his friend. He told the police that the men who attacked the two of them said, 'You cannot do a thing to us. We are the MLA's men'.

Explaining that they hit the victim with rods, Aslam said he heard them call out to each other by name. 'They were calling each other Suresh, Vijay, Paramjeet, Naresh and Dharmendra.... I got away but I saw them and heard them hitting Rakbar', Aslam said in a written statement as a key witness to the whole episode.

Even as he expressed his apprehension of danger to his life as also a regret for leaving his friend at the mercy of the attackers at the last minute, Aslam remains a vital cog in the investigations. How much his disclosure will mean is yet to be seen. After all, the dying declaration of Pehlu Khan

---

[31] Ibid.

in which he named the six accused was not regarded as enough evidence by the Rajasthan police to nail the culprits. Rakbar, like Pehlu, died in Alwar. Inevitably, the investigations too are being done by the police of the same state.

Several obvious questions hover unanswered. The victim was attacked around 12:30 AM; the police, informed at 12:40 AM, reached the spot some 35 minutes later at around 1:15 AM, by which time Rakbar was badly beaten, almost too shocked to say a word and too wounded to stand up. Yet, the police took him to a hospital located only 4 kilometres from the site of the crime after almost three hours. In between, as alleged by Nawal Kishore, they stopped to have tea and arrange a vehicle for the cows to reach a shelter. Worse, as stated by another witness, she saw the police beat an already thrashed victim who needed urgent medical care.

Were the policemen merely negligent of their duty? Did they not realize the severity of Rakbar's injuries, or was the police in collusion with the attackers, waiting for the victim to die rather than survive to relate the tale to the world? Were they trying to protect some of the attackers—particularly because two of the men immediately arrested were the ones who had themselves travelled with the injured in the police vehicle to the communal health centre? Were the two made scapegoats? The answers may never be found.

Meanwhile, Rakbar's family, never too far away from hunger, stares at an uncertain future.

> With no aid announced by the state government, Rakbar's father Suleiman Khan could not help exclaim, 'Lynch his seven children too as they would anyway die of hunger'.

Lynch Files

LENDING A HELPING HAND: Jamaat-e-Islami Hind's Khaliquz Zaman at the Home of Rakbar with His Daughters

Rakbar's Village Mourns Him

His wife, who was promised a new pair of earrings by Rakbar from the profit he would have made by selling more milk with two new cows, had to sell her only pair to manage a shroud for her husband for his burial. Unlike the politics outside, the family chose to give Rakbar a quiet, dignified burial where the chief imam of Ramgarh led the prayers. Incidentally, although Akbar, he was called Rakbar by a local dairy owner for whom he used to work. The dairy owner, a Hindu, used to worship a local deity called Rakbar, and decided to call Rakbar, born Akbar, by the same name. The name stuck, post death.

By the time Umar Khan (45) was lynched by cow vigilantes in Alwar, Rajasthan, some seven months after Pehlu Khan's murder in April 2017, the frequent instances of lynching had become international headlines. Pakistan's widely respected newspaper *Dawn* reported on Umar's killing:

Umar and Tahir
November 2017

> A Muslim man was killed and another left critically injured by 'cow vigilantes' in India's Alwar district of Rajasthan state.
>
> The two Muslim men were targeted for transporting cows in the same area where Haryana dairy farmer Pehlu Khan was lynched by a mob in April this year.
>
> A charged mob intercepted Umar Khan and his aide Tahir Khan when the two were taking four cows in a pick-up truck from Alwar to Ghatmika village in Bharatpur district. The mob allegedly harassed, assaulted and shot at the two men, resulting in the death of Umar Khan.
>
> To cover up the murder, the attackers allegedly threw Khan's body on a railway track. A train had run over the body when police found it. The remains were shifted to the Rajiv Gandhi Government Hospital in Alwar on Saturday.
>
> Khan's family approached the local police but were still waiting for registration of a first information report.
>
> The survivor, Tahir Khan, escaped from the spot. He was reportedly admitted to a private hospital at Ferozepur Jhirka in neighbouring Haryana.
>
> According to the media reports, the two men belonged to Meo Muslim community, which has a significant

strength in terms of numbers around the Mewat area spread over Rajasthan, Haryana and some parts of Uttar Pradesh.

The Meo community staged a demonstration and refused to accept the body from the hospital's mortuary. District Congress minority cell president Jamshed Khan, who was leading the protesters outside the hospital in Alwar, alleged that some policemen were already deployed at the crime scene but had not even tried to stop the attackers.[32]

The coverage of *Dawn* was a telling indictment of the space given to Tahir's killing by Indian newspapers. For most, it was a small item on page one, but details followed on the inside pages. For some, it was only a small single column news on the inside pages. The lack of space given to the latest lynching instances was not due to lack of brutality in the crime—here, the man lynched was thrown on the railway track to cover up the crime—but a certain degree of insensitivity setting in. Lynching a Muslim was not headline-grabbing stuff anymore. The frequent occurrence of the crime making many a journalist inured to it. Maybe, if Umar had been lynched before Pehlu, or even Akhlaq, there would have been a greater display of public anger, even media resentment. But Umar lost his life after our media had lost much of its initial rage. Lynching was almost the new normal.

So, what exactly happened with Umar and his friend?

Umar was travelling with his friends Javed and Tahir through Fahari village near Govindh Gadh in Alwar district of Rajasthan. They were transporting cows from Mewat in Haryana to Bharatpur in Rajasthan when they were assaulted by cow

---

[32] '"Cow Vigilantes" Lynch Muslim Man in India', *Dawn*, 12 November 2017.

vigilantes who, incidentally, had moved up a pace in the area in the run-up to Pehlu Khan's murder. They hit the men with sticks and clubs. Then shot Umar before throwing his body on the neighbouring railway track to make it look like an accident. The local Meo community, however, alleged that the crime was committed not just by local vigilante groups, but even the police was in collusion with the perpetrators. Demanding a high-level probe, Sher Muhammad, the chairman of the Meo Panchayat of Alwar, stated, 'The attack took place at around five in the morning. We are calling it a case of lynching too as they have not only been shot but also beaten up. We will press charges accordingly'.

However, there was an official attempt to project the victims as well as the attackers on the same page. While the Rajasthan home minister G. C. Kataria said that 'both sides are responsible' for Umar's murder—imagine a man inviting his own killing!—the police arrested two Meos and two Gujjars to show that this was a clash between two criminal groups and the police was being even handed. The police arrested Bhagwan Gurjar and Ramveer Gurjar for shooting Umar and inflicting a gunshot wound on Javed. Then came the expected, but provocative action for the victims. The police pressed charges against the injured men, and they were arrested on the charge of bringing cattle to Rajasthan from Haryana without valid documents. They were produced in a court in Sikar district and sent to judicial custody for two days.

At a conference organized by United Against Hate in New Delhi, Tahir's brother Maulana Abdul Wahid said, 'The goons (alleged cow vigilantes) are linked to the police. They throw stones to stop trucks ferrying cattle and then open fire. They steal the cattle and car parts before handing the vehicle to the police who register cases of cattle smuggling and harass the victims'.

'We want the killers of Umar to be punished. But now we are facing cases ourselves. The two boys who were with Umar—Tahir and Javed—were arrested on charges of cattle smuggling. The police have filed several such cases against our Meo community, including me', said Ilyas, who hails from Rajasthan.

The killing of Umar proved in unequivocal terms that the woes of the local Muslim community do not get over with the death, however, tragic or violent that might be, of one individual. The survivors have to start a long legal course to prove their innocence, and the families are financially enfeebled. The deceased is usually the head of the family, and his departure marks a straight tightening of the family finances, children dropping out of school, etc. Further, the family can no longer depend on earnings as a dairy farmer. There is too much risk involved, with the profession being de facto barred to Muslims in some parts of the country. For a Muslim to be seen with the cows is to invite trouble, even if he had been doing it for generations. For the injured, it is a long trek to courts at different levels to prove their innocence. The accused meanwhile either go scot-free or, as proved in other cases, have jobs and felicitation waiting for them after bail.

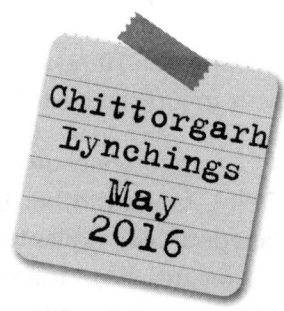

Chittorgarh Lynchings May 2016

In the age of 24×7 Internet, this news took time to travel. When it finally did, it was not courtesy any news channel or a national newspaper. Rather, the news seeped in through WhatsApp, bringing with it the attendant elements of doubt and suspicion. It was early June and Ramzan time in 2016 when the video of a man stripped to his bone being kicked by five young men made its first appearance. It seemed too

Lynch Files

vigilantes who, incidentally, had moved up a pace in the area in the run-up to Pehlu Khan's murder. They hit the men with sticks and clubs. Then shot Umar before throwing his body on the neighbouring railway track to make it look like an accident. The local Meo community, however, alleged that the crime was committed not just by local vigilante groups, but even the police was in collusion with the perpetrators. Demanding a high-level probe, Sher Muhammad, the chairman of the Meo Panchayat of Alwar, stated, 'The attack took place at around five in the morning. We are calling it a case of lynching too as they have not only been shot but also beaten up. We will press charges accordingly'.

However, there was an official attempt to project the victims as well as the attackers on the same page. While the Rajasthan home minister G. C. Kataria said that 'both sides are responsible' for Umar's murder—imagine a man inviting his own killing!—the police arrested two Meos and two Gujjars to show that this was a clash between two criminal groups and the police was being even handed. The police arrested Bhagwan Gurjar and Ramveer Gurjar for shooting Umar and inflicting a gunshot wound on Javed. Then came the expected, but provocative action for the victims. The police pressed charges against the injured men, and they were arrested on the charge of bringing cattle to Rajasthan from Haryana without valid documents. They were produced in a court in Sikar district and sent to judicial custody for two days.

At a conference organized by United Against Hate in New Delhi, Tahir's brother Maulana Abdul Wahid said, 'The goons (alleged cow vigilantes) are linked to the police. They throw stones to stop trucks ferrying cattle and then open fire. They steal the cattle and car parts before handing the vehicle to the police who register cases of cattle smuggling and harass the victims'.

'We want the killers of Umar to be punished. But now we are facing cases ourselves. The two boys who were with Umar—Tahir and Javed—were arrested on charges of cattle smuggling. The police have filed several such cases against our Meo community, including me', said Ilyas, who hails from Rajasthan.

The killing of Umar proved in unequivocal terms that the woes of the local Muslim community do not get over with the death, however, tragic or violent that might be, of one individual. The survivors have to start a long legal course to prove their innocence, and the families are financially enfeebled. The deceased is usually the head of the family, and his departure marks a straight tightening of the family finances, children dropping out of school, etc. Further, the family can no longer depend on earnings as a dairy farmer. There is too much risk involved, with the profession being de facto barred to Muslims in some parts of the country. For a Muslim to be seen with the cows is to invite trouble, even if he had been doing it for generations. For the injured, it is a long trek to courts at different levels to prove their innocence. The accused meanwhile either go scot-free or, as proved in other cases, have jobs and felicitation waiting for them after bail.

In the age of 24×7 Internet, this news took time to travel. When it finally did, it was not courtesy any news channel or a national newspaper. Rather, the news seeped in through WhatsApp, bringing with it the attendant elements of doubt and suspicion. It was early June and Ramzan time in 2016 when the video of a man stripped to his bone being kicked by five young men made its first appearance. It seemed too

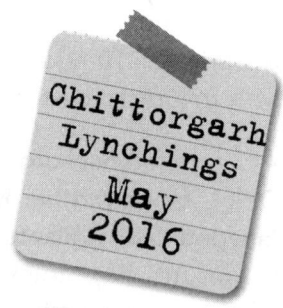

Chittorgarh Lynchings May 2016

bizarre, too cruel and shameless to be true. One had lingering misgivings about the contents. On careful scrutiny, it did not look morphed. It was a genuine case of a young man being assaulted by *gau rakshaks* with lathis, axes and swords in their hands. In the video, the victim was shown lying on the ground, probably a roadside field in Rajasthan with barely any greenery in the background. He was surrounded by his attackers, striking a menacing posture. Two of them had their foot firmly placed on his face. In one of the frames, one could see a policeman standing almost as a mute witness and, in another, a truck was in flames.

It was appalling, and seemed a clear case of complicity between the police and the murderers. Imagine a policeman standing watching a man being kicked around and taking steps neither to prevent the assault nor to arrest the men thrashing the victim. That was not all. Soon, the video went viral, being exchanged in hundreds of WhatsApp groups. It could be seen on YouTube too. Clearly, the men who had assaulted the driver said to be carrying cattle in his truck, felt fearless of the law. They had their political masters; they had their police and legal connections. They felt emboldened. Wearing saffron scarfs, hurling abuses, they wore smugness on their face, impunity their abiding feeling, and felt secure enough to own up the deed as an achievement. The helpless, almost dead, man at their feet seemed but a booty captured in war. Except that this was no war, not even a fight. Just a merciless attack on an unarmed man earning his living as a truck driver.

The national media never woke up from its slumber on the issue. Hindi daily *Patrika* from Rajasthan did carry a photograph of the attack and an accompanying report which seemed to have been put together from police dispatch. Hence, the driver was dubbed a cow smuggler; the men were not called arsonists or rioters or those attempting to kill a man. It was still some solace that the news did finally trickle into the media space. Then some newspapers finally picked up the item, but chose to confine it to a paragraph or two. It could as well have been a weather bulletin.

Only *Milli Gazette* carried a slightly longer report which was subsequently picked up by a handful of online forums, mostly catering to Muslim readers.

Incidentally, in the said case, a Muslim trader/driver and his three Muslim companions were intercepted by some goons, allegedly belonging to local Bajrang Dal and Shiv Sena, in the town of Chhoti Sadri in Chittorgarh district of Rajasthan. The truck was carrying cows and bulls. According to the police, it was carrying 50 cattle and was overloaded. As a consequence, four of the animals died on the way. It was intercepted on suspicion of cow slaughter by Bajrang Dal and Shiv Sena men. Three of the occupants of the truck, Rajender Chaturvedi, Manohar Kamawat and Dinesh Bawri, who all hailed from Pratapgarh, were attacked by goons. But they managed to escape with minor injuries. No such luck awaited their Muslim companions Ajju Hussain and others. They were dragged out of the vehicle, slapped, thrashed, stripped naked and kicked around. As the attack was on, one of the men made a video of the incident in which Hussain was seen as a helpless being almost half dead. He was later picked up by the attackers, and paraded naked along with his Muslim co-travellers around the town.

> Outrageously, even as Hussain was first attacked, then paraded naked, the police watched on, refusing to step in to stop the humiliation of the victim.

 Lynch Files

Worse, later cases were registered against the driver of the vehicle and two of his companions under the Cow Protection Act, Sections 3, 4 and 5. In its complaint, the police did not only mention the names of the alleged cow smugglers but also gave their father's name, and their religion as 'Muslim'. The animals were seized while the truck was reduced to ashes.

Later, the police also registered cases against 200 people for rioting and interfering in official work. Ranu Soni, Kailash Mali, Ravi, Sumit Sharma and Mukesh Mali were named among the accused. This was too much for the local population to take. The residents protested filing of the cases against local men and allegedly got the station house officer (SHO) transferred.

Shockingly, the local population had bought into the narrative of Hussain and his companions smuggling cow for slaughter. No evidence required, no knife discovered with the accused, no blade, just a mob pronouncing its judgment. When *Milli Gazette* approached the men who had left their phone numbers behind in the video, they expressed happiness at their 'accomplishment' and claimed that they beat the cow trader in such a way that he won't die but won't be able to sit or stand for months on end.

They succeeded to the extent of instilling fear in the victims who failed to pursue their case in the court of law. They were too scared to speak up, just relieved at being alive. Meanwhile, the *gau rakshaks* decided against resting on their 'laurels' and soon shared similar videos of their actions in Aligarh and Kanpur in Uttar Pradesh. The Frankenstein Monster unleashed with the lynching of Akhlaq had only just begun devouring the innocent.

The day was celebrated as Shaurya Divas, but really, there was nothing except ugly cowardice and deceit in the actions of Shambhulal Regar. But for his hideous deed on that day, Shambhulal would have been just another of unemployed, and maybe, unemployable youth of the country.

Rajsamand
AFRAZUL
6 December
2017

His gaunt frame, his loose-limbed ways revealing no sign of the hatred that lay concealed inside that frame; his eyes though were not his ally. A careful look at his eyes, and one could see traces of anger, even blind venom. His eyes gripped you, hatred brimming over. On 6 December 2017, his eyes ruled him as he called a small-time contractor and migrant labourer Afrazul on his mobile phone. Afrazul had been in Rajsamand for 12 years, having left his village in Malda, West Bengal, for greener pastures. Rajsamand did not offer him, and thousands of other migrant Bengali workers, stories of great success. What it did provide were two daily meals, which is something he could not be assured of back home. With his sustained hard work, Afrazul had married off two of his daughters while the third completed her education. He still lived in a rented accommodation though. In its own, silent way, his was a little success story, a little inspiration for penury-struck villagers in Bengal, that it was possible to step out of Bengal, and eke out a living. With his fellow migrants, he had carved out a little Bengal in Rajsamand; almost all his neighbours were Bengali, most Muslims too. Their interaction with the locals was almost entirely professional. They did a job they were hired for. They got paid. They went home happy for the day only for the struggle to resume the next day. Amid all this, there was never an occasion for local residents to pick up a fight with Afrazul. In absolute anonymity lay his peace and security.

Lynch Files

Then small-time marble businessman Shambhulal rewrote the script. Following Shambhulal's phone call, Afrazul went to meet him, matters of earning a living dominating his mind rather than recalling that on this day, 6 December, Babri Masjid was demolished in 1992. The media was occupied with talks on building a temple dedicated to Ram Lalla in Ayodhya; a few channels talked of Babri Masjid too. To the hungry Afrazul, food was god, and the phone call from Shambhulal offered hope of daily bread for a few days.

Shambhulal though had other ideas. With his 14-year-old nephew in attendance besides his little niece, the self-radicalized man attacked Afrazul, who was alone and caught absolutely unaware. It was on the pretext of business that he used to invite Afrazul over. Once there on a barren piece of land with some cactus plants and a few wild shrubs, Shambhulal all but beheaded Afrazul. His mutilation of a live man making for a most macabre spectacle. He did not stop there. He then set a crying, wailing Afrazul on fire. For a few minutes, he breathed in agony. Afrazul was about to die but Shambhulal had to stoop to another level yet. He asked his nephew to film the gory murder to upload it on Internet soon after. All along, Shambhulal ranted against the Muslim community, promising to eliminate them all. He wailed about Love Jihad, protecting the honour of Hindu women, and the like. It was a textbook case of hate violence and his own rant vowing to eliminate Muslims.

> Amazingly, for a few days, a section of the electronic media bought his lies on Love Jihad and tried to present the issue not as a hate crime, but one of passion.

Shambhulal is in prison and faces prolonged trial, and possibly a long time in the jail. With his brutal murder of Afrazul, however, he managed to stir local Hindutva leaders into action. Some right-wing foot soldiers spread a word around about his wife who was now left to fend for herself and the family, and promptly ₹3 lakh were collected for her aid. Local advocates stepped forward to fight his case for free.

A right-wing group took out a big rally in Udaipur in support of Shambhulal. More than 30 policemen were injured in a clash with hundreds of activists. Among the injured was the Additional Superintendent of Police Sudhir Joshi. The clash between the police and the protestors took place near Court Circle when the protestors unfurled a saffron flag at the entrance of the district and sessions court. Meanwhile, as reported by *The Indian Express*, the police in Rajsamand froze the bank account with deposits of around ₹3 lakh collected in the name of the accused. Police officers revealed that the money was donated by 516 people from across the country to the account being operated in the name of Shambhulal's wife, Sita. The police also arrested two businessmen for allegedly circulating images on social media of receipts acknowledging their donations to the account. The police crackdown followed an alert that a message was being circulated on social media with details of the bank account and an appeal seeking donations for the imprisoned man's family.

That did not deter Hindutva leaders from hailing Shambhulal's actions and hoping for a repeat soon after with the motive of driving the Muslim community away from the region. Recordings of the alleged conversations were spread through WhatsApp.

Threats were issued to Muslim bodies that had stepped forward to help Afrazul's family and sought security for other workers in the area. Two days after the incident, on 8 December,

 Lynch Files

organizations representing the minority community took out a protest march in Udaipur city. Around 3,000 Muslims marched peacefully. At the conclusion of the rally, they submitted a memorandum to the District Collector and demanded that action be taken against the accused. Not a stone was thrown. Yet things were simmering when the Hindu outfits took out a rally on December 14 in favour of Shambhulal.

The West Bengal Chief Minister Mamata Banerjee announced a compensation of ₹3 lakh for Afrazul's family besides promising a government job for one person from the family.

> I felt sad and hurt to learn about the incident in Rajasthan. A person was burnt alive. It does not matter whether the person was a Hindu or a Muslim. It is a murder of humanity. It is an inhuman and barbaric act. I spoke with members of the victim's family. The victim's wife was concerned about the future of her family members. I told her not to worry about it, we will address their concerns. It is our responsibility to help the family and stand by them. But who will give them justice? There are other migrant workers across the country. We need to help them fight the cases in court as they come from poor economic background.[33]

The Rajasthan Chief Minister Vasundhra Raje Scindia dubbed it a 'serious crime' and promised to provide justice to all. Soon, a CBI enquiry was ordered. The Prime Minister Narendra Modi preferred not to speak on the tragedy.

When the right-wing forces got to know of compensation, they collected some more money to finally notch up an amount

---

[33] 'Mohammad Afrazul Buried, West Bengal CM Mamata Banerjee Announces ex gratia', 9 Dec 2017, *The Indian Express*.

of ₹3.5 lakh for Shambhulal's wife. The Rajasthan government quietly handed over a cheque of ₹5 lakh to Afrazul's widow through Rajsamand Sub-Divisional Magistrate (SDM) Rajendra Prasad Agarwal.

Meanwhile, Afrazul's widow Gulbahar Bibi spends time in distant Saiyyadpur in Malda to mourn her husband's passing away. It was here that Afrazul was laid to her in the presence of nearly 2,000 people, all of whom had kind words to say for the departed. More than three months after Afrazul's brutal murder, Bibi had no idea why he was killed. Shambhulal had alleged that he was having a relationship with a Hindu woman. It was a claim she flatly denied, insisting her husband was a devoted family man. To her, Afrazul was a hardworking man, who worked so far away to bring up his three daughters. A little over two months after the tragedy, Bibi filed a plea with the Supreme Court that the enquiry be conducted by an impartial agency, and the videos of Afrazul's hacking be taken off from Internet. The apex court directed the CBI's counsel to take instructions based on the plea of Bibi. Through her lawyer, Indira Jaising, Bibi sought the appointment of a special public prosecutor for the trial, and transfer of the case to Malda district in West Bengal as the victim's widow lived there. The court agreed to look at the issue at a later stage.

Incidentally, Bibi's Saiyyadpur village provides a lot of labour to construction projects in Rajasthan. It is a place she would rather not have anybody else join.

Back in Rajsamand's Raj Nagar, Afrazul's merciless premeditated murder sent shivers down the spine of other immigrants. Most weigh their options: Is working in Rajsamand a good enough option despite the fear of gory death? Or, do the seedy lanes of Saiyyadpur provide an alternative with even more meagre income and severely restricted job opportunities? 'You know, the atmosphere in Mewar was different earlier. We have seen some good times. *Ab sukoon khatam ho gaya hai* [There is no peace of mind now]', said 77-year-old Manzoor Hussain Haji, sitting cross-legged at the Hussaini mosque crossing in Rajsamand town in an interview with *Frontline*. Haji did not spell it out, but his anxiety was palpable. He was referring to the recent brutal murder of a migrant worker in Rajsamand and the insecurity that minorities have begun to feel in Rajasthan.

HORRIFYING MUTILATIONS IN HARYANA

It was the night of the new moon in June 2017. At New Delhi's Jama Masjid, the mood was sombre. Not a sign of bright lights that illuminate many a mosque this evening, not much chat from devotees, ready to head to the market for last minute Eid purchases. It was all eerie and calm. It was then that the imam of the masjid, Muhibullah Nadwi, revealed the reason. 'A 15-year-old boy has died. Killed'. His voice failed him for a few seconds before he completed the sentence. 'He was hafiz (one who had memorized the Quran), heading home to Ballabhgarh after Eid shopping in Delhi. Killed on a moving train'.

Ballabhgarh JUNAID on Delhi-Mathura Train June 2017

A little more prodding and some research completed the picture. The hafiz was Junaid, 15-year-old son of Jalaluddin, one of the seven siblings. He had initially studied at a madrasa in Surat before moving to Mewat and was planning to become an *aalim*, a religious scholar. It would have needed sustained hard work for at least nine years, but his madrasa principal believed he had it in him to do it. After all, he knew many hadith like the back of the palm. And, unlike many boys his age, he steered clear of profanities in his speech, preferring instead to enlighten his peers with his knowledge of the tradition and practices of the Prophet.

Of course, he loved to fly kites and did not take it well if someone cut his kite. Like most boys in small towns of India, he never shied away from trying his hand at a game of gully cricket. And, like most boys, he considered himself an all-rounder, a guy who would like to bat first, bowl first and field like Jonty Rhodes. Films were a no-no, but he liked bikes and prevailed upon his elder siblings Hashim and Qasim to save money to buy a second-hand bike. Although usually seen in a spotless kurta–pyjama in his madrasa, and even in masjid, once in a while, he would indulge himself by getting into a pair of jeans with a t-shirt and sneakers. He was like any other guy, lacking neither in ambition nor the patience and hard work to fulfil it. Yet he was different. Soon after entering teenage, Junaid had memorized the Quran, thereby assuring, as a section of Muslims believe, a place in Paradise for seven generations of his family. His parents could scarcely have been happier. In the summer of 2017, Junaid had recited the whole book from memory in taraweeh, special prayers in Ramzan. On the successful completion of Quranic recitation, Junaid was showered with gifts. There was a feast of biryani in his honour where all the locals participated. Eid was just a few days away, and festivities were in the air. As a hafiz who had recited the Quran, Junaid was gifted ₹1,500 by the devotees, a sum they collected from well-wishers and regular namazis at the mosque. Junaid's joy knew no bounds. With the money, he wanted to buy toys for his eldest sister's three children. He wanted to buy a gift for his 12-year-old little brother too. And, maybe, just maybe, he could afford to buy himself a new pair of jeans.

Next morning, even as family members slept after the *suhur* (pre-dawn) meal, Junaid, along with his elder brother Hashim and two friends, headed to Delhi. Yes, Delhi is where his heart lay. It was a big city, with a big mosque, the grand old Jama Masjid in old Delhi. Junaid took a train to the capital and proceeded to Sadar Bazar area where he caught up with some of his old friends besides his early ustads (teachers). Then the four of them went to Jama Masjid. A trip to Delhi could not be complete without a prayer at the historic masjid. Some shopping followed, and Junaid, singing like a bird, moved to Sadar to catch a Delhi–Mathura train that would take him home in time for iftar (meal to break the fast). All was fair and fine.

Then it all unravelled. Junaid and his companions got into an argument over a seat with Naresh, Rameshwar, Chander Parkash, Gaurav and Pradeep.

[
The argument soon degenerated into a scuffle wherein the attackers called Junaid and his friends 'anti-nationals' and 'beef-eaters', pulled at their beard and threw their skullcaps on the floor.
]

Soon, Junaid's companions called up their friends and other family members who reached Ballabhgarh railway station. The incident took place barely 60 kilometres from Delhi near Asaoti in Haryana. Other passengers looked on with nobody coming forward to rescue the boys.

Lynch Files

The reports which appeared in most media channels were sketchy, ranging from a 'hafiz being stabbed aboard a train' to 'boy accused of eating beef, killed on Mathura-bound train'. The missing dots were provided by the All India Students' Association fact-finding team which went with comrades of CPI(ML). The team spoke to Hashim, Shakir, Junaid's brothers and others. Their report said it all. They quoted Hashim,

> It takes approximately 45 minutes to come to Delhi from Ballabhgarh in train. In the evening, after completing the shopping, all four of us were returning home by train. We had boarded the train from Sadar. The crowd in the train was slowly increasing. The four of us sat across each other in the train. After some time, a 70–80-year-old man got onto the train and Junaid left his seat for him so that he could sit. Pushing and shoving began in the train from Okhla station.
>
> Around 20–50 people had got in the train together from Okhla. Junaid was standing at this time and suddenly because of all this pushing and shoving he fell down on the floor of the train. Junaid and I requested people to not push. At this, someone from the crowd snatched my cap, threw it on the floor and crushed it with his feet. After this they caught my beard. When we tried to stop them, they started beating us. They started shouting that we are Muslims, anti-nationals and beefeaters.
>
> After this, the other people training in that coach also almost joined those people. Nobody tried to stop them. They were 10–15 of them and were beating us mercilessly. After the train crossed Tughlakabad

station, I called my brothers and informed them and they all came to Ballabhgarh station. However, when the train stopped at Ballabhgarh, these people did not let us get down. They had together held us four. After this, my elder brother Shakir and some other friends who had come to take us also got onto the train. They started beating them too. As soon as the train started from Ballabhgarh, one of them took out a knife. The knife had sharp teeth. He attacked Shakir with this knife. After attacking him with knife they were pushing him around. When Junaid and I went to save him, they attacked me and Junaid with the knife too. The next station was Asaoti about 10 minutes way. But within this time they had killed my brother Junaid.[34]

When the team was talking to Hashim, he was lying on the bed. He had also suffered knife injuries in several places—on shoulders, legs and feet. Shockingly, at the station too, nobody came forward to help a clearly bleeding Junaid and badly wounded brothers and friends. A neighbour saw them and informed Jalaluddin a few minutes before iftar. Initially, Jalaluddin did not know Junaid had died in the attack. It was only when he overheard his father ask somebody to make preparations for a coffin did the reality dawn on him.

Six men, including an employee of Delhi government, were arrested. A month later, one of them, Chander Parkash, was released on bail by the sessions court with the Additional Sessions Judge Y. S. Rathor dropping Indian Penal Code

---

[34] All India Students Association, *AISA – CPI (ML) Fact Finding Report on the Lynching of a Muslim Youth in Ballabgarh*, 25 June 2017, available at http://www.aisa.in/aisa-cpi-ml-fact-finding-report-lynching-young-muslim-youth-junaid-hailing-khandawali-village-ballabgarh/

Section 34 dealing with common intent behind a crime. It was argued that Parkash had no common intention with the principal accused Naresh. The Haryana Police withdrew charges of rioting (Section 146 of IPC), unlawful assembly (Section 149 of IPC) and common intention (Section 34 of IPC) against four of the six accused. It left Junaid's father disappointed. More so because Parkash, along with four others, had confessed to being part of the mob that harassed Junaid.

In an interim order, the additional district and sessions judge, Faridabad, rapped Additional Advocate General Navee Kaushik for helping the counsel of Naresh Kumar, the main accused, by 'suggesting questions to be put to the witnesses' at the hearings was helping the counsel of Naresh Kumar—the main accused in the Junaid case.

In November 2017, Kaushik was asked to resign following allegations that he helped the defence lawyer. A month later, in December 2017, Junaid's family filed a plea that the matter should be investigated by the CBI. Their plea was turned down as the CBI told the court that state police was equipped to handle the case, and a trial was on.

Later, Rameshwar Dass, an employee of Municipal Corporation of Delhi, got bail too with the Punjab and Haryana High Court stating that the initial dispute between the victims and the accused was 'only regarding the seat sharing and abuses in the name of castes and nothing more'.

This was the observation of Justice A. B. Chaudhari who passed the order on 28 March 2018. The order read, 'There is neither any evidence of any pre-planning to cause incident deliberately or intentionally or to create disharmony'.

Incidentally, a trial court had dismissed Rameshwar's bail plea saying that he 'was involved in the quarrel with the victims from the very beginning and had abused the victims in the name of their religion and did not allow the victim to alight the train'. But Justice Chaudhari overruled it.

> The incident sent shock waves across the country, leading soon to 'Not in My Name' campaign in 16 cities and towns in India and abroad as masses stepped out to denounce the killing under the name of Hindus.

Law Minister Ravi Shankar Prasad too described Junaid's lynching 'as extremely painful and shameful'.

Today, with Junaid gone, his brother Shakir, who was accompanying him on the train, recovers from his head injury after a long treatment at New Delhi's All India Institute of Medical Sciences. Another brother, Hashim, has taken his place as an Islamic scholar of the family. He is an imam at a local mosque in the village. Yes, the family is not giving up on keeping Junaid's legacy alive. His younger brother Adil, like Junaid, has been sent to a Surat madrasa to become a hafiz.

Hope he has better luck on completion of his studies.

A Mother's Never Ending Wait: Junaid's Grief-Stricken Mother

Mustain Abbas ran for dear life. As did his four companions as they were chased by BGRD members on the Shahabad–Delhi road. His companions proved more fleet-footed or luckier. They escaped the fatal clutches of cow vigilantes. Abbas was not. While running, his foot hit a stone, he stumbled. He got up and ran. It was the little time he took in getting back on his feet that proved fatal. Injured, he was nabbed by men who kill in the name of the cow. Abbas, incidentally, was coming back from Kurukshetra where he had gone to purchase cattle. He could not get cows. He settled for a bull to till his fields in Saharanpur in Uttar Pradesh.

Kurukshetra
MUSTAIN
ABBAS
March
2016

Knowing the dangerous times he was living in, Abbas had taken due precaution. Rather than travelling alone in surcharged times, he moved in a group, and did so in a Mahindra van. As Abbas moved towards Delhi, he found a road blockade with some tractors parked diagonally across the road. In the distance stood some 10–12 men, ready at a minute to fire. Sensing trouble, Abbas and co-travellers reversed their vehicle. However, barely had they changed directions that cow vigilantes fired at the tyres of their vehicle. As the tyres went flat, Abbas and companions stepped out and started running. In vain, it proved for Abbas. His friends reached home in the morning to break the news to his family.

However, more testing times lay in store for Abbas and family. Once captured, the BGRD members tortured him relentlessly. By the time 27-year-old Abbas breathed his last, he had injury marks all over his body. His father alleged he had sword wounds, shrapnel marks. The body was mutilated, a clear giveaway on the torture inflicted upon Abbas before he passed away. Worse, as the family claimed, they sought relief from two police stations on the route—Peepli and Shahabad—but no help came their way. Rather, they were advised to forget it as it could get worse. The cops were clearly keen to hush up the case and facilitate safe passage for the murderers. The family finally got relief when they moved the Punjab and Haryana High Court in March. The court ordered the transfer of the district magistrate and several police officers. In May, the CBI was asked to probe the issue. The state government opposed the view and sought the help of the Supreme Court in restraining the agency. The apex court refused to stay the investigation though the transfers of the police officers were put on hold. The CBI deputed a member to visit the aggrieved family. The family submitted details of the incident, but no arrests were made.

It was but a minor triumph for the beleaguered family. Life itself became a challenge after Abbas's death. The family had to wait for about a month before the confirmation of Abbas's death came via a phone call from Shahabad police station. The mutilated body, recovered from near a drain, came with marks of torture, each mark strengthening the resolve of his father and wife to fight on.

Incidentally, Abbas had four kids, the youngest of whom was merely two. Said to be an indulgent father, he would often make his youngest child sit on his shoulder as he ran around the house. Not very well off, he had borrowed money from his father to buy cattle, and ended up buying a bull to plough his fields.

LYNCHED AND FILMED IN UTTAR PRADESH

A little under three years after Akhlaq was lynched to death on the mere suspicion of killing a calf, the abominable piece of history repeated itself. Not in some remote corner of the country, but just 15 kilometres from Akhlaq's Bishara village in Dadri. This time the victim  was a 50-year-old Mohammed Qasim, a goat trader suffering from thalassemia, who was similarly lynched by a mob in Pilkhuwa's Bajhera Khurd village, around 50 kilometres from India's capital, also a distance covered by tempo from Dadri by many locals. He was not a cow trader. Rather, he had moved to Pilkhuwa more than two decades earlier to improve his financial prospects because of the township's proximity to New Delhi. Every now and then, he would procure goats from nearby villages and sell them in Delhi and other local markets at a profit. This was his way of sustaining his family of six children and a wife.

A few days before he was attacked by a mob on an allegation of cow slaughter, Qasim was visited by a man who asked him to buy his buffalo. Qasim agreed. And a little after Eid-ul-Fitr celebrations, he got a call asking him if he were still interested in purchasing the animal. Around 11:30 AM on the fateful day, Qasim stepped out of his house to buy the animal, making sure to carry a little extra money just in case he could strike a good bargain for a goat or two. He had with him around ₹60,000 for the purchase. He informed his son while going out. It was to be the last time Qasim walked out of his home or talked to a family member.

> Just a little later, he was attacked by a mob, his clothes torn apart, his body bruised, bleeding and thirsty. He died pleading for water, even as his assailants, including teenage boys, watched with a mix of amusement and triumph—hatred and jubilation writ large on their young faces.

Even as the boys mouthed expletives on Qasim for being a Muslim and a cow slaughterer, they made a video of it and uploaded it on social media soon after. Alongside, a photograph went viral.

The photograph captured the assailants dragging Qasim across the streets of the village with the local police in attendance. Two men held him from around the shoulders and armpits while his feet grazed along abrasive unpaved road. A cop was seen clearing the path ahead, while his colleague escorted the villagers dragging Qasim. Yet another colleague was seen engrossed on his mobile. Meanwhile, Qasim's barely covered body was dragged across the dusty path to be possibly dumped into the nearest pit. There was not a sign of a cow, dead or alive, or any meat anywhere in the vicinity.

A few hours later, another video surfaced which showed that Qasim was not the only man attacked by cow vigilantes. There was Samiuddin too. An old man in his mid-60s, Samiuddin was a farmer and had gone to collect fodder for his animals. He had sat down with his companion Hasan for a little smoke when he saw the mob attacking Qasim. He saw some 25 people rushing from Bajhera village to hit Qasim and attempted to rescue him. Even as Hasan fled the scene, Samiuddin tried to reason with the violent mob. With disastrous consequences, as he was to find out. The men soon transferred their attention to Samiuddin, greeting him with the worst expletives besides constantly hitting him, and calling him to confess that he was a cow killer. His plea that he was a farmer and that

DEAD AND BURIED: Qasim's Grave in Hapur, Western Uttar Pradesh

Lynch Files

there was no knife in his possession for possible slaughter fell on deaf ears, and Samiuddin was brutally thrashed—his leg fractured with lathis, his arms broken, his head bleeding and his beard pulled at as an attack on his religious identity.

In the video that went viral soon after, Samiuddin is seen bleeding, being repeatedly pushed, shoved, slapped, kicked and abused. He is called a cow killer by cow vigilantes. The old man pleads ignorance, mildly remarking that he had killed no cow. So distraught was Samiuddin when he was thrown outside the Devi temple as the mob believed he would die soon that he had to be admitted to the ICU of a local hospital. He later recalled to the Press how the local police handled him and Qasim without any sensitivity.

Samiuddin could hear the cops tell each other that Qasim was dead, and that the other man (Samiuddin) is likely to die too. As luck would have it, Samiuddin spent around three weeks in various hospitals in Hapur and Delhi before being discharged—his arms in casts, his right leg in a plaster. During this time, his statement was not taken by the police. 'They came once or twice to the hospital when I was in ICU. Sometimes, I was only semi-conscious and not in a state to give a statement. They never came to me after I recovered my consciousness', Samiuddin told the media in Delhi, adding that he felt in danger for having spoken out against the police.

Referring to the attempt to camouflage the violence as a case of road rage, Samiuddin said,

> The mob called me mullah. They pulled at my beard. They spat on me. And claimed they would teach me a lesson. Where does a bike figure in such talk? They grabbed me by the shoulders and grabbed me by the collar. They hit me so hard that I fell down.

They hit me more asking me to stand up. Qasim was behind me. Sometimes, they would hit him, sometimes, they would hit me. (Interview with India Against Hate activists)

The killing of Qasim and the indignities and cruelties visited upon Samiuddin sent shock waves across the region and reminded many of Akhlaq. The fears, as it turned out, were not misplaced. There were chilling similarities between the two.

> Like in Dadri, the local Muslims alleged, the lynching of Qasim and Samiuddin was a planned affair with the local temple being once again used to rally the villagers. An announcement of cow killers being nabbed in the village was allegedly made from a local temple, consequent to which the locals gathered at the temple.

A little before the alleged announcement, a rumour had spread in the village that some cow smugglers were trying to steal their cows to butcher them. Qasim, and particularly Samiuddin with his flowing white beard, were easy targets, a couple of Muslims in a village dominated by Hindu Rajputs.

Later, Qasim's brother, Saleem said in a media interaction in New Delhi: 'They killed my brother because he was a Muslim. There could not have been any other reason. He had no knife, no axe, nor did he have a cow'.

He revealed Qasim was attacked by more than two dozen young men, who circled him, almost like a group of lions pounce upon a helpless deer. Then they assaulted him with lathis, thrashed, slapped and kicked him until he almost died. And when he was about to die, he pleaded for water, an action which was filmed by the mob. Yet the men chose to deny him a sip of water.

Later, Qasim's younger brother, Mohammed Sheikh asked, 'Take a look at the video. You will see how he was thirsting for water, much like a fish thirsts for water when out of it. Can such a man slaughter a cow? And if so, where is the animal or its body?'

The question begs an answer, except that the local police was not able to find one. Initially the police attempted to dismiss it as a case of road rage wherein there was a clash of two bikes and the riders lost their cool, leading to a violent altercation. It is a version fiercely contested by the families of Qasim and Samiuddin as also others from the village, who claim they were forced to sign on the FIR as a condition for meeting the victims. Qasim's brother Nadeem said,

> Our family was informed around 3:30 p.m. that my brother Qasim was admitted to a hospital as there was a fight between him and some other people. We were asked to come to the police station. We were kept waiting there till around 6.30 p.m. before we were informed that our brother was admitted to a local hospital. With great difficulty did we find the hospital, only to find Qasim dead, and most of the Rs. 60,000 which he carried were missing. There was only an amount of Rs. 14,000 left. (Interview with India Against Hate activists)

The version of the police was contested by Samiuddin's brother Yameen too. According to him,

> It was a fabricated story that a sick man and an old man were found slaughtering a cow. Neither had a knife. Nor was there any sign of the animal to be slaughtered. The issue of the cow slaughter was raised merely to murder them and incite a communal riot. (Press conference by Samiuddin's family members in New Delhi)

Although the police discovered neither a cow nor a bike, local men of Bajhera Khurd are clearly seen in the video, and have been identified by the victims' families. Samiuddin himself recognized five of the attackers. Indeed, Samiuddin's family found ink marks on his thumb, giving rise to suspicion that, in a semiconscious or unconscious state, his thumbprint was taken on a blank sheet of paper on which the FIR was later written.

Samiuddin's brother Mehruddin contended that his brother was attacked merely because he tried to save Qasim.

> My brother had gone to collect fodder for his cattle when he saw some boys beating up a man. He tried to intervene. Upon this the boys called up more men. Soon there were around 40 men who attacked my brother, but we were informed by the police only around 3.30 pm that he had been admitted to a hospital. However, we were not allowed to meet him till about 6.30 pm. When we finally managed to see him, there was no part of his body which did not bear a mark of injury. And there was an ink impression on his thumb too. (Interview with India Against Hate activists)

It is alleged that during the 3-hour period, from 3:30 PM to 6:30 PM, the police asked the family to sign on the FIR already written. Dinesh Tomar, a friend of Samiuddin, claimed that the police dictated the FIR according to their convenience. He said, 'Write the report as I tell you. Otherwise, you and your family, and also Samiuddin will be behind bars for cow slaughter. You know whose Government it is'.

It is only when the families of the two men attacked by cow vigilantes signed on the papers that they were allowed to see them. Too late, as it proved for Qasim's family.

The version of the two families gave further credence to the feeling that the police deliberately misled them as far as filing a complaint is concerned. It was only when the videos of the twin assaults went viral that provisions of attempted murder, rioting, etc., were added by the police after the botched attempt to turn a clear case of lynching into one of road rage relating to a clash of motorcycles. Contrary to the official version, no bike was found lying at the scene of the crime. The police arrested four men, including Yudhisthir Sisodia, for the crime. Later, non-bailable warrants were issued against 11 others.

However, the day Samiuddin was discharged from the hospital, the first piece of news that greeted him was that Sisodia, the key accused in the lynching tragedy, had

Qasim's Son Shows the Only Photograph of His Father

File 2: Muslims: Easy Targets?

Men Assemble Outside Qasim's Residence to Share Their Grief

been granted bail by a sessions court. Indeed, a sessions court in Hapur had granted the bail on submission of a bond of ₹1 lakh.

Samiuddin spent 20 days in hospital; Sisodia spent the same time in jail. Apart from him, three others, Rakesh Sisodia, Sonu and Kanu, were arrested. It left the Uttar Pradesh police red-faced. Having earlier apologized for the photograph showing three policemen escorting the alleged attackers of Qasim as they dragged his body, the police claimed that they had filed the case under strict provisions.

Superintendent Sankalp Sharma said,

> A person accused under Section 302 (murder) of the IPC normally doesn't get bail easily. I can't afford to comment on the court order but we had put together

the statement of the victim's family, video footage of the incident and other corroborative evidence in the case diary.[35]

It cut no ice with the local Muslims who believed the cow was once again being used as an instrument to fuel hatred against the community. The cow was a political, not a sacred animal. Further, the timing of the two incidents gave rise to feelings that the idea was to instil a sense of fear in the community in the run-up to and around Muslim festivals: Akhlaq was killed immediately after Bakrid celebrations, and Qasim likewise butchered to death soon after Eid-ul-Fitr festivities.

However, the fight for justice goes on. Following the sessions court bail to Sisodia, noted human rights lawyer Vrinda Grover stepped in to fight the case at higher levels of the judiciary. 'We will fight the case till the highest court to get justice to the victims', she said. Even as the fight was on, Sisodia was caught in a sting operation by news channel NDTV boasting about the killing. 'They slaughtered cows, so I slaughtered them', he is reported to have said. NDTV reported that Sisodia claimed he was not scared when he went to jail and was given a hero's welcome when he came out of prison. He claimed that around four cars came to take him home and people were raising slogans in his name, which made him feel proud.

The Supreme Court took notice of the sting operation and agreed to hear the petition filed by lawyers of the victims. It also ordered the Uttar Pradesh Police to provide security to the sole survivor of the attack, Samiuddin.

Clearly, the last word is yet to be said in the case.

---

[35] 'Hapur Lynching: Main Accused Out on Bail, Victim's Kin Say Cops Diluted Case', *The Times of India*, 9 July 2018.

File 2: Muslims: Easy Targets?

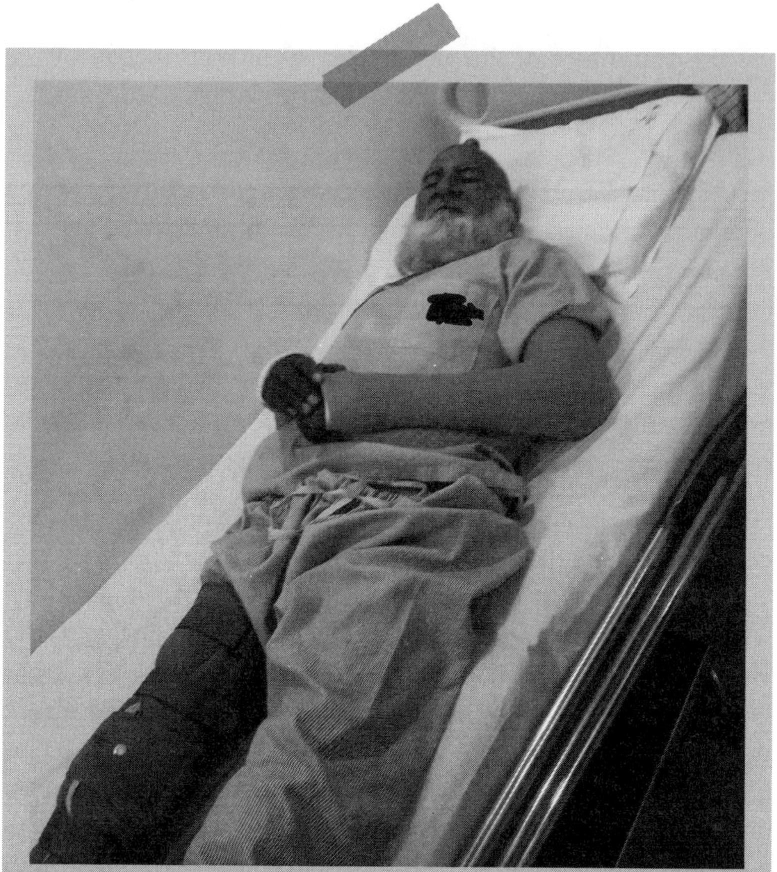

LUCKY ESCAPE: Samiuddin Recuperating in a Delhi Hospital

HANGED BY THE MOB IN JHARKHAND

Two images stay in the memory of any Indian when the name Ramgarh is mentioned. The first image goes back to 29 June 2017 when Alimuddin Ansari, a 45-year-old man from the neighbouring Manua village, was forced to pose for the camera after he was mercilessly thrashed by a mob that accused him of carrying cow meat in his Maruti van. In the picture, one can see the hands of a man in red T-shirt and black pants, holding up Ansari's face for the camera. Clad in blue jeans and an unbuttoned blue shirt, Ansari is clearly helpless. In an adjacent picture, his much-loved Maruti van is reduced to ashes in front of his eyes. Ansari's picture brings to mind the photograph of another man with folded hands pleading for his life in Gujarat 2002.

Ramgarh
ALIMUDDIN ANSARI
June 2017

Cut to early July 2018. One year later, Ramgarh is back in the public eye. There is a new image of the township doing the rounds. This time we have the BJP leader Jayant Sinha garlanding eight men convicted of killing Ansari. The felicitation comes soon after their life sentence is suspended by Jharkhand High Court on 29 June 2018, exactly a year after the incident.

> A fast-track court in Jharkhand, on 21 March 2018, had awarded 11 *gau rakshaks* a life sentence for the 29 June 2017 murder of Alimuddin Ansari in Ramgarh. These included the BJP district media in-charge Nityanand Mahto. The convicts later got bail in the high court.

Incidentally, back then, Ansari's widow Mariam Khatoon had melted many a heart by saying she was against the death penalty for her husband's killers, and a life sentence was sufficient.

The men in the picture seem pleased to get sweets and garlands from the Harvard-educated Hazaribagh MP of the ruling party.

The first picture had brought tears to many eyes. And sensitive beings were driven to outrage, with many well-known civil rights activist like Harsh Mander making a stopover at Ramgarh and spending time at Ansari's residence with his widow and sons as part of his Karwaan-e-Mohabbat expedition. That the killing came within hours of the Prime Minister Narendra Modi's address at the Gandhi Ashram in Sabarmati—where he said that 'killing people in the name of gau bhakti is not acceptable. This is not something Mahatma Gandhi would approve of'—only added a touch of wistfulness to the whole tragedy. Was the prime minister so helpless?

Were the goons so defiant? And what about the leaders of his party?

Sinha's picture exposed him for what he is: a dubious politician who weighs the pros and cons of a decision based on electoral politics. He was apparently perturbed due to a local BJP leader who claimed credit for organizing bail for the convicts and stood to lose Hindutva votes if not saved by something as dramatic as garlanding them. With one stone, he killed two birds: at one level, he reiterated his Hindutva image and at another, he easily outsmarted local BJP leaders in the competition for a possible lead role in the party in future.

It was reported by the media that following the high court judgment granting bail to 10 of the 11 convicts, there was a scramble between the supporters of former BJP MP Shankar Chowdhury and Ramgarh district BJP President Pappu Bannerjee, who owed allegiance to the Minister of State for Civil Aviation Jayant Sinha. On the day, Bannerjee outsmarted his party rivals, bundled the eight men just released into his vehicle and brought them to Sinha's bungalow where the minister was waiting for them with flowers and sweets, and posed happily for pictures with them.

It is another matter though that Sinha's action did not go down well with educated Indians with a clear set of rules and values. For them, the men garlanded by the minister were not just accused but convicts. Many of them were seen in the video and photographs which they themselves had uploaded of Ansari's killing. A minister honouring cow vigilantes or convicted murderers given bail until pendency of the case was just not acceptable. Although Sinha later issued a clarification on Twitter, stating he believed in non-violence and the rule of law, the image had been cast in stone. It did not help that he never went to condole Ansari's death or establish contact with the victim's family which is part of his constituency.

The photographs, one year apart, kept the Ramgarh incident simmering. Yet, if one looked carefully, Ansari's killing set a template for the future. Almost a year after he was lynched to death, the killing was followed to the last letter by the mob in Hapur where Qasim paid with his life. Indeed, the template for Qasim and Samiuddin's case in Uttar Pradesh was laid in Jharkhand. Like in Hapur a year later, the victim in Ramgarh was a family man in his 40s. He was neither well educated nor very well off, just happy to meet the requirements of his family. Some day he was a coal merchant, others he was happy to play the driver if somebody needed to travel. On still other days, he picked up passengers on his van. And, somehow, managed to look after his family's needs. Here too a crowd of cow vigilantes pounced on a lone Muslim man and did not rest until he had breathed his last. In both cases, the police did everything possible to delay, to procrastinate, even obfuscate.

If in Hapur, the relatives and friends had to run from one hospital to another, from a police station to a nursing home, then another, for around three hours before they were able to see the victims; in Ramgarh, things were a little worse. Here, the family of Ansari first went to the local police station in Ramgarh around 11:00 in the morning. The police, however, decided to undertake a cruel exercise in deflection. Instead of informing the family about Ansari's fate, a policeman took his wife to a government hospital to get her on a drip as she was allegedly feeling weak! This bought the police a few hours, before finally in the evening, around 6:00 PM the family was told the truth. Ansari was no more. Lynched in daylight in front of around a hundred men.

 Lynch Files

So, how did it all start in Ramgarh? Well, the local Bajrang Dal members had been on an active mode for a few weeks before Ansari's killing. WhatsApp messages were exchanged, and provocative speeches and slogans aired in public. The idea was to instil fear in the Muslim community. Among those accused of murdering Ansari were members of the Bajrang Dal besides a local cow-protection group, the BGRD. On the day he was murdered, Ansari, a coal merchant, and not a cattle trader, as said by a section of the Hindi and English media, left home in Manua around 8:00 in the morning. A little later, his van was intercepted by a mob at Bazartand in Ramgarh district. Soon, he was dragged out of his van and lynched by around 50–100 people; 12 men were mentioned in the FIR filed later. Ansari's van was also reduced to a burnt mangled mass. Ansari died before he could be taken to a hospital in Ranchi.

In the video which was circulated, Ansari is not seen fighting his assailants and trying to be aggressive with them. In fact, he maintains calm even when an attacker violently snaps his head towards the camera for a better picture. He only pleads to be let off. All along, the attackers are cheered on by a crowd that possibly included shopkeepers in the vicinity. Pertinently, no meat is seen being taken out of the van though there is a pile of it on the road. How it got there, which animal's meat it is, is not answered.

The same video reached his 16-year-old son Shahbaz who switched on to it out of curiosity like any teenager, only to discover that the man being lynched in the video was none but his father. He immediately took his bike in an effort to reach the spot to save his father. Unfortunately, his driving skills were at best elementary, and he soon fell down a little distance from his house. He called his elder brother Shahzad who left with his mother for Ramgarh market. On reaching there, they found their car burnt and turned upside down, and the stains of Ansari's blood on the road. They were told that he had been taken to a hospital by the police. On reaching the Ranchi hospital, they discovered that Ansari had succumbed to his injuries. By then, it was evening.

According to police, however, the officer-in-charge of the Ramgarh police station was informed around 9:45 AM that a Maruti van carrying prohibited meat was set on fire by a mob. On arrival, the police found that the vehicle had been burnt, and two packets of meat in plastic bags were lying there. Also lying injured was Ansari who, according to the officer-in-charge, admitted to carrying prohibited meat. A case was instituted under Section 414/34 of the Indian Penal Code, Sections 12(2) and 12(3) of the Jharkhand Bovine Animal Prohibition of Slaughter Act, and Sections 11(D)/20, 21 of the Prevention of Cruelty to Animals Act against the unknown (victim). According to police, Ansari was first taken to a local hospital in Ramgarh but transferred to Rajendra Institute of Medical Science where he breathed his last.

As no immediate arrests were made of those seen clearly in the video, some local boys protested. However, the police slapped harsh charges on them, resulting in a jail term for many of them. Meanwhile, 11 arrests were made for the lynching of Ansari. The case continued to be heard in the fast-track court. However, before the court could conclude its proceedings, another woman paid with her life for daring to try to help the Ansari family.

At one hearing in October 2017, one eyewitness Jalil Ansari was due to appear before the fast-track court. As he had forgotten his identity card at home, he sent his wife, along with Alimuddin Ansari's son Shahzad, on a bike to fetch it. Along the way, the bike was hit, allegedly, in a planned manner. Jalil Ansari's wife died on the spot while Shahzad sustained serious injuries.

Eventually the fast-track court found 11 men guilty and awarded them life sentences. Only for the accused to get bail three months later, and for Sinha to celebrate with flowers and sweets.

Mariam waits for justice; her little children having dropped out of school, her elder son left dumbstruck by the tragedy. Today, he has given up all ideas of studies and works as an

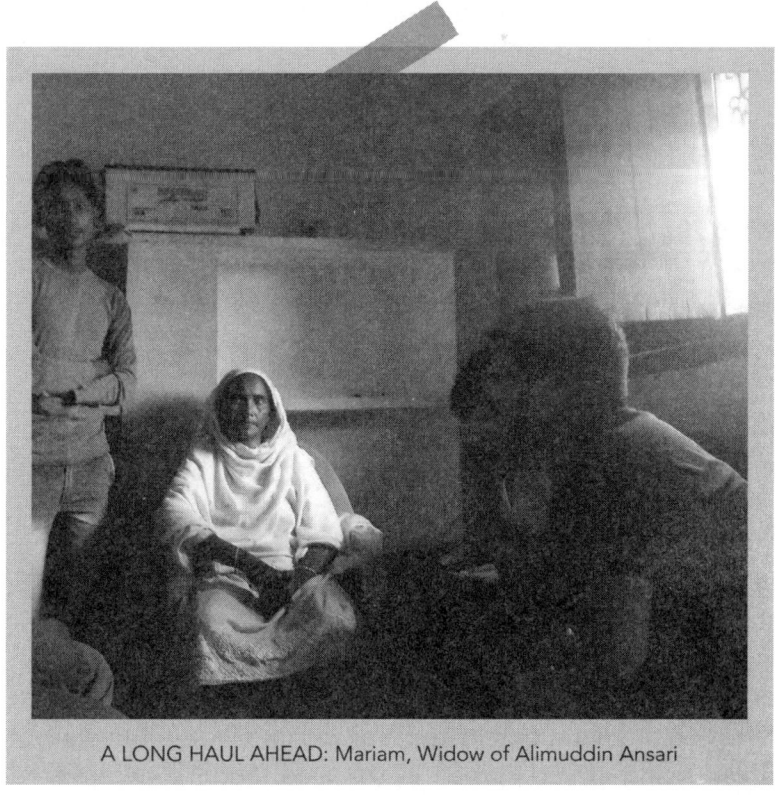

A LONG HAUL AHEAD: Mariam, Widow of Alimuddin Ansari

electrician to look after the family. Mariam did get ₹2 lakh as compensation from the state government but little else, no job for self or children. Today, besides the meagre earnings of the elder son, the family is dependent on the goodwill of the community. Some community elders help out with a token sum every now and then.

> Worse, she runs around for her husband's death certificate. As he is said to have died on the way from Ramgarh to Ranchi, the authorities are not able to decide under whose jurisdiction did he breath his last.

As they pass on the buck to each other, Mariam waits, unable to lay hands on her husband's bank account, not even able to apply for widow's pension. In official record books, she is not a widow. In reality, her husband passed away more than a year ago. Meanwhile, Sinha takes stock of his political gamble.

Giridih
USMAN
ANSARI
June 2017

If ever Akhlaq's lynching in Dadri proved a precursor for similar assaults in the country, Usman Ansari's lynching in Giridih comes the closest in almost total replication, except for the positive role played by the police in the latter instance. Rest there is an eerie similarity. A lone Muslim family in a Hindu-dominated Barwadah village. Rumours of a calf being slayed spread in the area. Soon a decapitated cow is found in the vicinity. Ansari pronounced guilty by a thousand-strong mob without giving him a chance to present his version of events. Within no time, he is called a cow killer, and the mob attacks his house. Ansari is mauled; the neighbours thrash him until they take him to be dead. Then they set his house on fire.

Then there is twist in the tale: Just as they were about to set a presumably dead Ansari aflame, there arrived a district commissioner and local police. Ansari is rescued in the nick of time, literally saved by seconds. As the district commissioner drives him down to a hospital, the van is stoned by the crowd. Ansari is somehow taken to a Hazaribagh hospital where his condition is pronounced precarious. His bones are reduced to pieces, his pulse is low. His head is badly swollen. He is unconscious. He stays that way for eight days before starting a long process of recovery which is completed two months later at a Dhanbad hospital. His physical wounds are attended to, but his mental scars remain. It is unthinkable for him that his neighbours set out for him, that it is they who attacked him and burnt his house. He struggles to come to terms with the reality, but decides to go back home or whatever is left of it. He is advised against it; he won't be safe there anymore. Yet, Ansari wants to go back to his home. Maybe because he has an innate bond with it. Maybe because he has nowhere else to turn to.

When he was in the hospital trying to get back on his feet, his family's financial fortunes took a hit. All the medical expenses took a toll, and the family had to resort to borrowing from relatives. Soon, that avenue for help dried up, and Ansari's sons had to go to various mosques and ask for alms from namazis (devotees) to meet his medical expenses. One son, in this traumatic phase, lost his mental balance. No neighbour stepped forward to help in peaceful times, just as hardly anybody had tried to stop the mob when it stepped out to set aflame Ansari and his house. Yet Ansari stayed determined to go back to his home and hearth. He remained away from strangers for a long time, his family members not even sharing their phone numbers with unknown people. After being discharged from Ranchi hospital, Ansari stayed indoors, too scared to step out. The mental scars clearly needed more time. Gradually, his condition began to improve, even if only slightly. He recalled the events of the fateful day in a media interaction, 'It was June 25, 2017. My cow was not keeping well for some time. I tried tending to it, but failed. The animal's condition deteriorated. The calf passed away. We dumped the body at designated place for dead animals, and tried to get a sweeper to dispose it off. However, we could not agree on a price to be paid for the disposal of the dead animal', his voice trailing off (Informal interaction with India Against Hate activists). The missing dots were filled by noted civil rights activist Harsh Mander who managed to meet him on his Karwaan-e-Mohabbat expedition after sustained efforts. He found a man broken in body and spirit. Mander wrote in *The Indian Express*,

> He reared 10 cows and sold milk to both Hindus and Muslims. Some 10 days before the attack, one of his jersey cows fell ill and died. The custom of the village is that dead cattle are not buried but thrown in a designated yard. Ansari contacted the man from a disadvantaged caste who usually disposed (off) dead cattle. But they could not settle on a price. So Ansari decided to drag the corpse with his sons to the dumpyard, where it lay for two days. The day of lynching, two days after Eid on June 27, the corpse was found mysteriously without its head and leg. Rumour

spread that Ansari had killed his own cow to eat during Eid. A mob surrounded his home baying for blood. A terrified Ansari pleaded that the cow died of sickness. If he had wanted to eat her meat, why would he take away its head and leave the body which contained the meat?[36]

However, his words fell on deaf ears, as the mob proceeded to drag him, strip him and thrash him before going to lock up his son and daughter-in-law inside a room at the house and set it on fire. They escaped courtesy a local guard who broke open one of the doors, enabling them to flee.

Usman Ansari, a Giridih Lynch Mob Attack Survivor, Still Loves His Age-old Home

---

[36] 'Usman Ansari, Like Mohammed Akhlaq', *The Indian Express*, 20 September 2017.

The police arrested five persons, and one man was injured in the fire as the mob stoned the vehicle in which Ansari was transported to the hospital.

> Later, much like Dadri, there was no remorse among the neighbours. Nor was there an attempt to equivocate or to parry off questions. Yes, they had lynched Ansari. He deserved to be lynched was the cry of the young and the old.

On being told that Ansari yearns to come back to his house, that the area still has some sentimental value for him, they demanded that first he should take back the FIR filed against the attackers, the police should free the men arrested for the crime, and Ansari should refuse to recognize anybody who attacked him. The poison of hatred ran deep. For them, even after Ansari's departure from the locality, and a miraculous escape, he continued to be guilty, the man who had provoked the Hindus by eating a dead cow. That he had lived among them for decades, and, in fact, grown old with many of them was of no consequence. That he had never had a quarrel with any villagers, that he had never slayed any of his animals meant nil. On that fate day in June, soon after Eid celebrations, Ansari was a cow killer. Dadri could well be Giridih, and Mohammed Akhlaq could as well be called Usman Ansari.

And pray, how different was the role of police, otherwise accused of favouring the attackers? Well, in this case, the police rescued Ansari and his family. Soon after the successful rescue operation, a senior police officer R. K. Mulik said,

> Our men braved the crowd and immediately rescued Ansari and his family members. When the police tried to take him to the hospital, there was resistance from the crowd. There was heavy stone-pelting. We had to open fire in the air. Two men were injured in the police firing and around 50 policemen injured in the stone-pelting. (Press statement issued by the local police)

It was also discovered that somebody had slit the throat of the dead animal to prove that the animal had been slaughtered by Ansari. The innocence of the victim was established.

Latehar MAZLOOM ANSARI and IMTIAZ March 2016

In April 2018, an international collective of 11 organizations including New York-based Alliance for Justice and Accountability, Lucknow-based Rihai Manch, Mumbai-based Citizens for Justice and Peace, and New Delhi's Jamia Teachers' Solidarity Association released a report which exposed official apathy, and even hinted at collusion, in the Latehar lynching of Mazloom Ansari, a 32-year-old cattle trader, and 12-year-old boy Imtiaz who was accompanying him. The report indicted the Jharkhand Police in no uncertain terms. It said, 'Despite eyewitness accounts, a positive post-mortem report, confessional statements and corroborative evidence, Jharkhand Police unable to prosecute people who hanged cattle traders'. Such strong words had great potential to cause a political storm. Yet, it was buried in single-column or two-column stories on the inside pages of most newspapers in New Delhi, Kolkata and Chennai. Only *National Herald* gave it ample space and a prominent display. For others, probably, lynch fatigue had begun to set in after reams devoted to the killing of Akhlaq some six months earlier. Maybe, it was indifference to a tragedy which took place far from the gaze of metropolis India. Unlike Dadri, no editors could drive down in a couple of hours from their posh offices in New Delhi to Latehar's Balumath village. It was a sleepy little place that presented a clear disconnect between India and Bharat. Either way, Ansari and Imtiaz were denied their rightful place as victims of majoritarian intolerance masquerading as false religiosity of self-proclaimed *gau rakshaks*.

The collective's report, however, did a good job of exposing loopholes in the entire episode of lynching of Ansari and Imtiaz in the wee hours of 18–19 March 2016 as they set foot to go to a cattle fair in the vicinity. What happened from thereon was a classic case of modern-day rumour mongering through WhatsApp messages, mobile phone conversations and arrogant youth smug in the tacit understanding of being above the law. The report noted,

> Though Gau Rakshaks' attacks had already shot up since Prime Minister Narendra Modi came to power in May 2014, this killing was the first to meet the classic definition of a 'lynching'—hanged by a mob—originating in the racist history of the U.S. where for centuries White supremacists lynched thousands of Africans, Latinos and even native Americans.[37]

---

[37] 'Latehar Lynching: Jharkhand Police lets Murderers Get Away', available at: https://www.nationalheraldindia.com/india/latehar-lynching-jharkhand-police-lets-murderers-get-away

 Lynch Files

The report added later, 'Neither the Government of India and nor the Government of Jharkhand has condemned the hangings and the Gau Rakshaks. No compensation has yet been made to the victims' families'.

On the day, Mazloom and Imtiaz set out with their eight oxen for a local cattle fair where they hoped to make a good profit by selling the animals. They had bought the animals a fortnight earlier from a local fair and brought them to Dumatand where Mazloom's in-laws stayed. The plan was to reach the fair early. Hence, the two started on foot around 2:30 AM, walking the animals in the dead of the night. Imtiaz's father Azad and another friend and business partner Nizamuddin followed them on a bike. Azad had fractured his leg earlier; hence, his son Imtiaz was chipping in for him. After a little distance was covered, Nizamuddin fell behind Mazloom and Imtiaz. This little separation proved fatal as it was during this time the cow vigilantes struck, assaulting Mazloom and Imtiaz, hurling abuses, all the time beating them with belts, canes and rods. Soon Azad joined him and heard the cries of his son who had been abducted by then. They reached the spot and found both Mazloom and Imtiaz missing, but their oxen very much there. Nizamuddin called up Munawwar, brother of Mazloom, who too joined them. They soon reached the spot in Balumath where Mazloom and Imtiaz were being strung by a rope. They hid in the distance and watched in horror the killing of their near and dear ones.

By morning, the word spread of the hanging of the two. The villagers blocked National Highway 99, demanding immediate arrest of the culprits. They attacked Balumath police station too. A few days later, the government announced a compensation for the victims' families which was turned down because it had allegedly come too late. Instead, Mazloom's wife demanded stringent punishment and arrest of the guilty.

File 2: Muslims: Easy Targets?

Later, in his deposition before the court in January 2017, Imtiaz's father Azad gave a detailed eyewitness account of the attack. He told the court that after he had covered some distance from his residence in Latehar, he heard his son's screams for help. He followed the voice and saw a group of people armed with pistols, abusing and assaulting Mazloom and Imtiaz. He hid in the bushes. 'I saw Arun Saw had climbed a tree and was fixing a rope. The others were on the ground trying to push Mazloom and Imtiaz up to hang from the tree'.

Thus, in front of Azad, Nizamuddin and Munawwar, Mazloom and Imtiaz were hanged to death by cow vigilantes in Latehar.

As fear struck the Muslim homes, villagers in Balumath decided to make themselves heard through protests and dharnas. However, shock awaited them. The local police, instead of arresting the accused, turned its ire on the protestors. Many were injured and cases were filed against 10 men, all Muslims. The men have since been on the run.

Like in other cases, the police tried to portray the incident as an accident on the road, involving a 'simple road robbery'. However, later, S. P. Anoop Birtharay conceded, 'The manner of their hanging showed that the assailants were led by extreme hatred'. Last word was yet to be said in the whole sordid saga. The autopsy report went public. In it, Dr Laxman Prasad and Dr S. K. Singh, both government doctors, clearly stated that 'long, hard, rod-like, blunt' weapons were used in attacking Mazloom and Imtiaz, putting to rest the earlier contention that it was a simple road robbery. Then came another controversy with the release of the collective's report. The NGOs' report revealed attempts to hush up the case.

> The failures of the police, deliberate or otherwise, began as soon as the crime ended. It is stunning that

though the crime occurred during 3.30–6 a.m., the police registered the First Information Report (FIR) nearly 17 hours late, at 10.47 p.m. Incredibly, even the autopsies had been carried out before the FIR was registered. Nowhere does the FIR explain this delay.[38]

Further, it was contended, 'during the trial that started in August 2016, neither the prosecution nor the presiding judge expressed any concern over this lapse or asked for an explanation'. Also, Nizamuddin had in his statement to the police identified Vinod Prajapati, a local BJP leader in Latehar, as one of the perpetrators of the crime. However, despite his contention, Prajapati was not called for interrogation. The response of the police to Nizamuddin's statement is nothing short of negligent. Although, Vinod Prajapati was named in the FIR.

> In fact, Prajapati isn't even standing trial even though the other eight men, not named in the FIR, are. The charge-sheet filed in May 2016 included elaborate confessions from all the eight accused. Not only did they detail the crime, they also detailed their actions hours prior to the murders, establishing that the crime was premeditated. Yet, despite the fact that under the Indian Evidence Act a confession made to a police officer is not admissible as evidence, the police made no effort to get these confessions recorded before a magistrate under Section 164 of the Criminal

---

[38] 'Latehar Hangings: Justice Denied as Accused Gau Rakshaks Roam Free', available at: http://www.catchnews.com/india-news/latehar-hangings-justice-denied-as-accused-gau-rakshaks-roam-free-106324.html

Procedure Code (CrPC), which would have made them admissible as evidence.[39]

The fight goes on for justice. But it is a fight that is taking a heavy toll of the victims' families. At every hearing, the accused 'appear in the court as heroes. They come with around 200 supporters, while most times we are all alone, just our family members', as Munawwar told a website TwoCircles.Net. It does not end there. With the accused getting bail, there is danger to life and limb of the victims' near and dear ones. Mubarak Qureshi said to the media,

> Arun Sahoo, the main accused in the Latehar incident and a member of the right-wing extremist group, Bajrang Dal, has in the past held a pistol against my head and threatened to kill me. They asked me for a ransom of Rs 1 lakh and when I refused, I was taken to the nearby jungle where I was beaten to near death.[40]

Adding that the attackers had the audacity to call up the police and instruct them to 'finish us off'. 'The police did not kill me and took me to a hospital. I was admitted in Ranchi Institute of Medical Sciences (RIMS) for 15 days, but the police refused to even register an FIR in the matter'. Similarly, harrowing has been the experience of Hashim Qureshi. A little more than a year ago, he and two of his friends were coming back to

---

[39] Arraigning a Person as Accused not Named in the FIR or Charge Sheet – Section 319 Code of Criminal Procedure, 1973. Available at: https://www.legallyindia.com/views/entry/arraigning-a-person-as-accused-not-named-in-the-fir-or-charge-sheet-section-319-code-of-criminal-procedure-1973

[40] 'Two Years after Latehar Lynching, No End in Site to the Terror of "Cow-Vigilantes"', available at: http://twocircles.net/2018jan25/420257.html

 Lynch Files

Balumath after purchasing cows for breeding and rearing. On their way, about 15–16 people attacked them. 'Shamim, the driver of the vehicle, was hit on his head with a blunt instrument. We were then taken captive and taken to the side of the road to be lynched'. Fortunately, a passerby alerted the police who arrived at the spot. 'But even then, the police refused to arrest the perpetrators of such a crime. These are the same people who in March 2016 killed Mazloom Ansari and the minor Azaad Khan (Imtiaz)'.

Azad Khan, Father of Imtiaz with Nadeem Khan of India Against Hate, on His Way to the Court

KILLINGS IN THE NAME OF THE COW

Jammu: Sammi

This incident came on the heels of the lynching of Pehlu Khan in Alwar, Rajasthan. Somehow, it failed to evoke the same level of indignation, the same sorrow. Maybe distance from Delhi was a contributing factor. Although fatigue with hate violence had not yet set in, the Jammu tragedy failed to get similar space in the media. While the print publications consigned the story to a small space on the inside pages, the electronic media too mentioned it only in passing. But truth be told, the lynching of a nomad family over suspicion of cow smuggling deserved as much condemnation and as much media space as came the way of Pehlu and his family members. The brutality was relatively less, but the consequences were equally devastating. It was particularly devastating for the entire tribe as nomads because of the very lifestyle were put on notice for future. If it could happen to one family on the move, there was no guarantee it would not be repeated.

The modus operandi was largely similar to other similar preceding and succeeding instances. A Muslim man/family on the move with cows; rumours of cow slaughter or smuggling; no evidence, no proof, nothing. A mob lying in wait, a targeted assault on the innocent on mere suspicion of smuggling or slaughter, and an FIR which mentions no names. Once again, the police going soft on the perpetrators of the crime.

Here, a mob of 200 people attacked a nomadic family in Jammu's Reasi district on the suspicion of cattle smuggling. Five persons, including the family's 9-year-old girl Sammi, were injured, the girl ending up with multiple fractures.

The family was crossing a stretch in Reasi's Talwara area. They were taking along their goats, sheep, horses, dogs and cattle. The presence of so many animals should have been sufficient proof that the family was one of nomads and was moving with all members, human and animal, in search of fresh avenues of livelihood. In fact, a large number of nomad families are seen on the move in April every year in these parts of the country. Yet, it did not turn out to be a sufficient insurance, as it was during this stretch that the family was attacked by cow vigilantes. Some of the attackers had iron rods. The family was ill-equipped to handle the onslaught of the so-called *gau rakshaks*.

Later, the police filed an FIR. 'We have arrested persons involved in the attack on the nomad family moving with their livestock—cattle, sheep and goats on April 20 night', a senior police officer told a news agency. The police too claimed that the attack on the family was 'a clear-cut case of misunderstanding and no cow vigilante group was involved in it'. Yet the police failed to prove how the mob came to attack this family, and attacked no other family using the same stretch of road at that time. Other families too moved with their animals, including cattle and horses.

One of the victims, a family member of Sammi, said,

> They beat us ruthlessly. Somehow we managed to flee from there. One of our children, a 10-year-old, is still

File 2: Muslims: Easy Targets?

missing. We don't know whether he is alive or dead. They even beat our elders very badly. They wanted to kill us and throw our bodies into the river.[41]

Little Sammi complained, 'They didn't even spare dogs. They too were taken away'. The mob seized the entire livestock of the family, including horses, goats, sheep and dogs, besides 16 milch cows.

The attack on Sammi and her family members reminded some locals of another incident of cow-related violence. Back in 2015, Udhampur was rocked by protests after a petrol bomb attack on a Srinagar-bound truck by some right-wing activists. Then too the activists attacked the vehicle on mere suspicion of cow transportation. The gruesome assault on Sammi faded from public memory only when a much more ferocious attack on 8-year-old Ashifa took place in Kathua. Being second in tragedy, however, did not exactly act as a balm for Sammi. The girl needed sustained medical treatment before being able to cope with the demands of a nomadic lifestyle.

Hours after 28-year-old daily wage earner Noman had been lynched to death by a blood-thirsty mob at Sirmaur in the Sarahan area in October 2015, a spokesman of the BJP in Himachal Pradesh blamed the ruling Congress government for abetting cow smuggling in the state,

Himachal Pradesh
NOMAN
October 2015

---

[41] 'Gau Rakshaks Attack Nomad Family, including 9-year-old girl, in Jammu and Kashmir's Reasi, say reports', available at: https://www.indiatoday.in/india/story/gau-rakshaks-attack-nomad-family-jammu-kashmir-972923-2017-04-22

and not doing enough to curb illegal cattle trade. 'Hundreds of cows roam the street in the state. They are smuggled to Uttar Pradesh by cow smugglers', he alleged. It did not strike him at all that this was a case of hate crime, an occasion when the masses killed a man in full public view, against all rules and norms. Noman may or may not have been trading legally in cattle, but the mob certainly lynched him. No wonder, Imran Asghar, Noman's relative, in a telephonic chat with *The Hindu*, asked, 'You can't kill people like this. What has happened to this country? Even if he was found to be with cows it does not mean that you would lynch the person'.

The game of political brinkmanship continued even as Noman was buried at Saharanpur in western Uttar Pradesh, with the Congress leaders in the state calling for immediate arrest of the culprits. That there is a difference of a daylight between enlightenment of speech and darkness of deeds became apparent when the state police arrested four men who accompanied Noman, namely, Nishu, Salman, Gulzar and Gulfam. The four men had been thrashed by the mob too. They were booked under different sections of the Cruelty to Animals Act. The truck was impounded as well. The attackers were not nabbed. Political quarrels continued, but a youth had life snuffed out of him, while four others were booked even as their attackers roamed free.

Odd and questionable but it was on the cards ever since a mob gathered at Lawasa Chowki on Sarahan–Chandigarh road on the intervening night of 14 and 15 October after Bajrang Dal activists lodged a complaint with the police about the smuggling of cows and calves. And a truck coming from Malerkotla in Punjab on its way to Saharanpur was intercepted by the mob and cops; the irony of the policemen standing with an aggressive crowd lost on all. On seeing cops and crowd, the five men in the truck ran towards adjoining forests, leaving the cattle to roam free. While others escaped with multiple injuries, Noman was thrashed to death. A case was registered under Section 302 of the Indian Penal Code against unknown persons for his death. Later, the police explained to the media, 'When the truck driver threw the cows on the road, people chased the occupants who tried to hide themselves in the forest', adding, 'all the accused are from Rampur village in Saharanpur district of Uttar Pradesh'.

Again, the irony of the usage of the word 'accused' for victims did not strike the policemen. Nor indeed did it strike them that the dead man could be an honest trader in cow, a mere transporter of animals or a dairy farmer. None of which can be substituted by the expression 'cow smuggler'. Thus the tables were turned, the men who should have been protected by the police from a threat or possible assault by people determined to take the law in their own hands, being called as an accused of the crime. Importantly, at no stage was the alleged crime proven. And those responsible for killing a man not proved guilty by any court at any level—the mob played the aggrieved party as also the judge—were taken as law-abiding citizens whose religious sentiments were hurt by the men in truck.

> **Although it was among the first lynching instances following the murder of Akhlaq, the reactions of the local police and politicians proved that nothing had changed or was going to change. Interestingly, the same expression 'cow smuggler' was used by the police in the lynching incidents in Jharkhand in 2017, Alwar in 2018.**

Even the RSS ideologue Indresh, tasked with bringing the minorities closer to the fountainhead of Hindutva, could not resist drawing a parallel between beef eating and lynching. In a statement to the press, he said, 'Such incidents will stop when Muslims give up beef eating'. With a single sentence, he made the victims the accused, those who provoke lynching with their dietary habits and gave an easy alibi to those who kill in the name of the cow. Worse, there was an element of threat too: continue eating beef, and lynching will continue. It did not amount to just an attempt to control the dietary habits of a community, but was a covert threat: fall in line or risk being eliminated.

Meanwhile, Noman's family in Saharanpur's Behat area pleaded innocence and complained, 'It is poor people like us who get lynched. Nothing happens to big people'. This emotional statement said a lot between the lines. Indeed, why is it that the well-off people are never booked for assaulting poor dairy farmers and traders in the name of cow protection? And, among those who trade in cattle, why is it that the mob lays its hands on the poor, the law enforcement agencies too file charges against them alone? While some like Nishu and Salman are booked under various provisions of the law and face many years in jail merely because they happened to be transporting cattle from one town of India to another. Others, as in the Dadri case, are not allowed to rest in peace after death either. Remember how the FIRs and forensic science laboratories' reports changed in Dadri, how mutton became beef, etc.? And how the family which lost its head in the mob attack was itself turned into an accused a year later? Or the police reports in the Pehlu Khan case a little later? Not to forget the reluctance of the authorities to give a death certificate to the family of Alimuddin who was lynched in Jharkhand more than a year after his life was criminally and cruelly cut short?

Also, do cow killers enjoy impunity with the law catching up with the cow traders fast, but turning a Nelson's eye to the vigilantes? Amid all the allegations and counter-allegations, it is the family of the deceased which suffers for no fault. The government confines itself to token condemnation with several conditions attached. Remember Indresh's supposed condemnation of cow vigilante's murderous attack on cow traders?

NORMALIZING LYNCHING

Until 2017, Maihar town in Madhya Pradesh was a picture of harmony. Known as the hometown of sarod legend Ustad Alauddin Khan, the town was never in news for any communal riots or bomb blasts. Life was peaceful. Its Muslim percentage was only 10 per cent of the population, but that never emboldened the local majority community to attempt to browbeat the minority. The two communities were happy to talk to each other rather than talking at each other. Even an occasional interfaith marriage failed to rouse tempers in either of the communities.

Satna
SIRAJ
KHAN and
SHAKEEL
17-18
May 2018

Then it all began to change in December 2017. Ustad Alauddin Khan's town took leave of its symphony to slide into a diatribe of 'we' and 'they'. It began with the celebrations of Prophet Muhammad's birthday in a Muslim colony of the town. The celebration was allegedly disturbed by some Hindutva groups. The Muslim community had to cut short its celebrations for the fear of violence getting worse. Meanwhile, a march by a Hindutva group was allegedly disturbed by some local Muslims, resulting in an altercation. The police arrested 10 people from both communities to bring the situation under control.

However, things were never the same again. The Hindutva groups retreated from the streets of Maihar but launched into a cyberwar, spreading unsubstantiated messages on WhatsApp about cows being killed by Muslims in the area. The messages had the desired impact: People who had never distrusted their Muslim neighbours began to doubt them. The Muslims, in turn, developed suspicions of their own. Tactics of polarization had succeeded even though the town had remained peaceful even during the Partition. With seeds of doubt well sowed, the town hurtled on the edge of communal strife. It came with the alleged killing of a bull by Siraj Khan and his friend Shakeel. Siraj was done to death by the villagers while Shakeel received serious injuries.

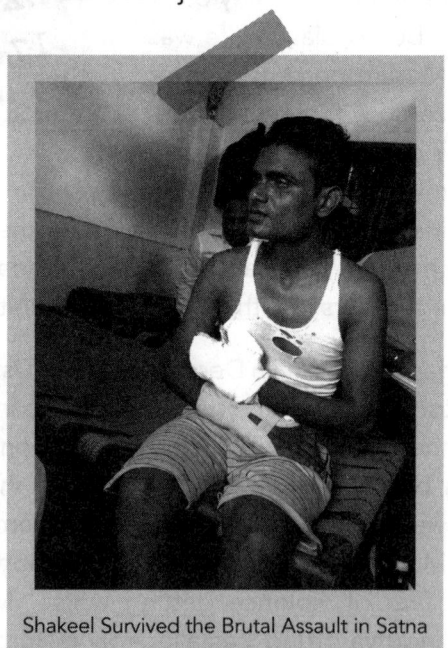

Shakeel Survived the Brutal Assault in Satna

The police was called. However, the police chose to file the first case against the dead victim of hate crime, Siraj Khan, initially erroneously called Riyaz Khan. Siraj and Shakeel were charged with cow slaughter. Even as the police waited for Shakeel to recover in hospital before arresting him, a second case was filed. This time against the four attackers, the men who assaulted Siraj and Shakeel. The attackers were charged with murder, and attempt to murder for the incident that took place on 17 May 2018 in Anjar village of Madhya Pradesh. The police booked the dead man and his friend under the provisions of the Madhya Pradesh Cow Slaughter Ban Act, 2004, and the Madhya Pradesh Agriculture Cattle Preservation Act, 1959. According to the police, the four accused— Pawan Singh Gond, Vijay Singh Gond, Phool Singh Gond and Narayan Singh Gond—were villagers from Amgara. They allegedly got to know that two men were slaughtering a cow in Anjar village, reached the site, 70 kilometres off Satna. There, they thrashed Siraj to death while Shakeel was left battling serious injuries in a hospital in Jabalpur. And the police waited for Shakeel to recover to arrest him!

Incidentally, according to the media reports, Siraj and Shakeel were walking back home in Maihar town of Satna district when they were stopped by a group of men in Amgara village. The two men were then 15 kilometres away from home. The men who intercepted them, soon called over more friends. It became a mob against two men. They accused the two of killing a cow, and beat them with lathis and wooden planks. The police claimed to have recovered a slaughtered bull, not cow, from the place. Siraj is survived by his wife, and four children, all between the age of 4 and 14 years.

However, the families of the deceased, as indeed some local Muslims alleged, there was another angle to the controversy.

Apparently, a local Hindu man owed Siraj some money which Siraj had gone to recover. Unable to pay up, the man turned the issue into a communal one rather than a quarrel between a moneylender and a borrower. It was a new ruse: turn an economic offence against a minority member into a cow slaughter case. Lynch the moneylender, and claim he was killing a cow. It was in some way, a step further from Haryana where cows seized from the minority community on the pretext of cow slaughter are distributed among the members of the majority community. So killing a Muslim on allegation of cow slaughter is a win-win situation for some *gau rakshaks*, often jobless, and short of cash.

> In the Satna instance, Siraj's family also alleged that the police registered a case against them without conducting a forensic test, and wondered how the police could come to the conclusion of cow meat after merely looking at meat.

However, as reported by the media, a forensic expert from Nanaji Deshmukh Veterinary Science University, alleged, 'It is impossible to identify beef without conducting forensic test, laboratory test or DNA test. Nobody can identify it, even veterinary doctor or physician. Moreover, if anyone goes through this process, at least three to four days will take to come to conclusion'. The law under which Siraj Khan, 45, (deceased) and Shakeel, 38, were booked was amended by the state government in 2012. As per the amended law, the maximum punishment of cow slaughtering is seven years

imprisonment with a fine of ₹5,000 which was earlier three years of imprisonment and ₹5,000 fine.

In the absence of widespread hue and cry over the lynching of men, it was left to Jamaat-e-Islami's Secretary General Salim Engineer to draw attention to the fatal wrong being committed. Wrote Engineer,

> We condemn the lynching of Siraj Khan. Media reports suggest that he was mercilessly beaten to death on suspicion of slaughtering a bull. This is absolutely unacceptable and shameful. There must be someone who must be held accountable besides the 'lynch-mob' as there seems to be no end to this series of lynching men from the minority community on charges of slaughtering bovines or possessing beef. (Salim Engineer at Jamaat-e-Islami headquarters in Delhi)

He drew attention to the usual way of defaming a minority community member, dubbing him a cow smuggler or a cow killer, then attacking him. Engineer further said,

> The usual modus operandi of those who are supervising these hate crimes from the background is to first kill, then glorify the killers, frame charges against the victims and ensure that there is no condemnation by anyone from the government. This attempt to 'normalize' lynching over the beef issue is most sinister and is extremely damaging for the country. (Salim Engineer at Jamaat-e-Islami headquarters in Delhi)

Amid all this, Home Minister Rajnath Singh visited Satna two days after the incident of lynching. He, however, decided against visiting the place of Shakeel or Siraj. The Chief Minister Shivraj Chauhan kept mum too; his silence easy to be taken as approbation of the action. Local television channels did not make it their prime news of the day. Hindi newspapers either presented the police version of the events or consigned the incident to the inside pages, much like a bike having a collision with a state transport bus. The English newspapers with their head offices in New Delhi could not care much either. Satna victim was denied even half the space that came the way of Akhlaq, or later even Pehlu Khan or Afrazul. The masses had become increasingly indifferent by the time of Satna tragedy; the media too sensed the mood. Lynching of Muslims became almost the new normal. Once lynched is forever forgotten.

The inhuman lynching of Pehlu Khan and his fellow travellers reached the national capital in a ripple effect. In South Delhi's posh belt of Nehru Place–Kalkaji, three men, in their 20s, were lynched for transporting buffaloes in the presence of policemen who later dismissed their injuries as 'very minor'. Never mind that each of the men needed to be admitted to All India Institute of Medical Sciences Trauma Centre, from where they were discharged the next day. One of the victims was seen with a bleeding cut below his eye.

Delhi
RIZWAN, KAMIL and ASHFAQ
22–23 April 2017

The men, Rizwan, Kamil and Ashfaq, were transporting buffaloes in a truck from Pataudi in Haryana to Ghazipur in East Delhi. They had their documents in order.

All was fine as the truck had cleared a good distance when it was intercepted by some 20–30 men near Kalkaji Mandir. Two men, Saurabh Gupta and his brother Gaurav, chased down the vehicle and dragged the truck occupants out around

Lynch Files

midnight. According to an eyewitness, in the presence of policemen, they started raining blows on the transporters. They stopped only when they saw Rizwan lying 'dead' on the road. Incidentally, Rizwan recalled the Pehlu lynching at that moment and pretended to be dead to save his life. He succeeded as his attackers took him to be dead and stopped thrashing him. This little act saved his life.

Not a person stepped forward to help Rizwan, Ashaf or Kamil. Around 11.45 PM, the police got a call from animal rights activist Gaurav Gupta and an emergency van reached the spot. There they found the truck with buffaloes parked by the roadside. The policemen thought it fit to arrest the attackers on the spot and seize the truck.

Later, the police stood in patient wait for the injured to be tended only to arrest them. They had been charged for cruelty towards animals. They were later released on bail. The attackers, meanwhile, were asked to cooperate with the probe. A little later, Delhi Police arrested Gaurav, said to be a member of People for Animals (PFA). Gaurav was released within hours of arrest from Kalkaji police station. The police recorded his statement. He told the police about his associates and how he had been tipped off about illegal cow transport in the city. Gaurav and his fellow attackers alleged that they had been chasing the truck from Basant village and succeeded after many kilometres at Kalkaji Mandir. He also claimed that he had not attacked the buffalo transporters, but it was done by the mob which had gathered at the place. 'It was not a matter of illegal transportation of cattle but carrying them in a cruel and inhuman manner,' deputy commissioner of police Romil Baaniya later told the media.

PFA denied that the attackers were on its rolls. This despite stickers on the attackers' cars being from PFA. The organization denied that it issues car stickers and promptly took off the men's name from their website. The NGO working for animal welfare denied any involvement with the crime. As reported by *Hindustan Times*,

> However, the PFA denied any association with the incident. Union minister Maneka Gandhi is one of the founding members of People For Animals and is also its chairperson. 'We have no PFA unit in Delhi. We have 10,000 volunteers across the country. Whoever acted did so in his individual capacity,' Gandhi's office said.[42]

Incidentally, Gaurav and his brother had been active in filing FIRs in similar cases in the past too. Before the Kalkaji assault, they had filed three FIRs where Gaurav gave his address as '14, Ashoka Road, New Delhi 110001'. It is Ms Gandhi's official address. He also produced an identity card which bore Ms Gandhi's signature and called him PFA 'officer Wildlife Crime and Cruelty Cell'. However, the authenticity of the card could not be established.

Irrespective of the involvement or non-involvement of any NGO activists in the Kalkaji lynching incident, the case sent shivers down the spine of the residents of the capital. Until the attack on Rizwan and others, lynching, in their view, was something which happened on deserted highways, far from the madding crowd. To them it happened when some men transporting cattle were assaulted by people, including the local goonda element, in the countryside. It could not happen in the heart of Delhi. Although there was no fatal injury, the case proved that lynching had reached India's capital and needed urgent attention. For too long, the cow militia was taking

---

[42] 'Three Men Transporting Buffaloes Beaten up in Delhi by 'Animal Rights Activists', *Hindustan Times*, 24 April 2017.

Lynch Files

refuge under matters of faith to dish out what it perceived to be justice. The non-state actors had enjoyed a free run ever since first Mohsin Shaikh and then Akhlaq were done to death. It was only with the Delhi incident that the local residents, otherwise well read, and well heeled, realized the tragedy of the issue. Tackling alleged *gau rakshak* assaults, noted activist and veteran journalist John Dayal wrote in *Dismantling India: A 4-Year Report*,

> The fact that the vigilantes 'do the job' is very convenient for the rulers. The state is not guilty of violence since this violence is allegedly spontaneous, and if the followers of Hinduism are taking the law into their hands, it is for a good reason—for defending their religion. The moral and political economies of this arrangement are even more sophisticated. The state cannot harass the minorities openly, but by letting vigilantes do so, it keeps majoritarian feelings satisfied. The private armies, which may be useful for polarising society before elections are also kept happy—not only can they flex muscles, but they usually exhort money (violence mostly occurs when they cannot do so, as is evident from the recent cases of lynching).[43]

Noted social activist Noor Mohammed made a similar point after a spate of lynchings in and around Alwar when he stated that most people could buy their way through. But those unable to buy their safe passage had to pay with their life. Noted academic Ashok Swain, quoted by Dayal, wrote,

> The present regime's political philosophy of Hindutva professes a pro-lynching ideology and promotes

---

[43] John Dayal, 2018, *Dismantling India: A 4-Year Report*.

pro-lynching discourse. Mob rule plays a key part in the strategy of Hindutva politics of social control. Lynching by the mob is not to punish a crime, but to enforce inter-group control, and to keep the idea and practice of upper-caste Hindu domination. In this context it does not matter whether the victim is guilty of wrongdoing or not—the lynching serves a larger political purpose.[44]

The capital's attempted lynching case proved each of the assertions and misgivings correct. Here were men transporting buffaloes, not cows, driving across Delhi with valid documents and receipts. Indeed, without them they could not have entered the city from Haryana, yet being hauled up by self-styled animal activists. And the police, instead of coming to the rescue of the men facing physical violence, filed a complaint against them and later arrested them. So, having documents for travel with cattle was not sufficient. It did not matter whether the victims, as Swain said, were guilty of wrongdoing or not. They were perceived to be wrongdoers by a group that claimed to be animal lovers. That is what mattered. Further, Rizwan and others were punished by the mob not for a crime but to assert dominant religion, dominant caste control.

The fact that there were more buffaloes than should have been accommodated on the truck seemed their only crime. Unless, of course, one believes that they happened to be just the wrong guys to transport cattle at that time in India.

Unfortunately, urban India merely blinked with this assault. It needed many more Pehlus and Qasims before the reality hit home.

---

[44] John Dayal, 2018, *Dismantling India: A 4-Year Report*, New Delhi.

 Lynch Files

File 3
The Mob Now Targets Dalits

AT THE MERCY OF UPPER CASTES

Hamirpur
CHIMMA
October 2015

In April 2016, noted academic Romila Thapar delivered the eighth Dr B. R. Ambedkar lecture at New Delhi's Ambedkar University. In her talk, she stated that stratified caste-based society had existed in India for millennia. The appearance of untouchability could be dated back more than two millennia with the appearance of the word *asprishya*. Calling 'permanent exclusion' of people based solely on birth worse than slavery because in the latter, under some given conditions, one could hope to buy one's way to freedom, there was no such option for one born 'untouchable'. Birth, not deeds, decided the fate. The worst of the lot were the Chandalas. Our ancient scriptures talk of severe strictures for one who is found eating with them, or establishes sexual relations with them. Incidentally, the oft-quoted Manu too spoke of Chandalas in terms of their possible descent from a union of a Shudra father and a Brahmana mother. It was said that the Chandalas deserved nothing new or pure; they ate leftover food, wore clothes taken of the dead and were allowed to wear only iron ornaments. Of course, under no circumstances were they allowed to enter the temples, and only in dire hunger could a *dwija* (twice born) accept food from a Chandala.

One had read these things in history books in school and believed that with the coming of the Constitution of India, such things were consigned to ancient days. Not so, one realized when a 90-year-old man was brutally attacked for trying to enter a temple said to be the sole preserve of upper castes in Uttar Pradesh's Kanpur area. The man, identified as Chimma, had gone to Maidani Baba temple for a *darshan* with his wife, son and younger brother. The family was on its way to Gaya. He was, however, prevented from entering the temple by one Sanjay Tiwari who believed that Chimma had no right to enter the temple and his stepping there would pollute it. The upper caste man claimed monopoly over the deity and the temple.

He initially shouted at the old man, before slapping him hard due to which he fell on the ground. Not content with this, Tiwari then got hold of a pickaxe to hit him. At this, Chimma's wife screamed for help, urgently trying to get onlookers to restrain Tiwari before it was too late. Desperate to act quickly, Tiwari then doused the old man in kerosene and set him on fire.

[
All this while other devotees at the temple in Bilgaon, located on the boundary of Hamirpur and Jalaun near Kanpur, watched in silence. No man or woman came to the rescue of the family which was left alone in screaming in protest and crying for help.
]

The police arrested Tiwari after some locals had nabbed him after he had killed Chimma. Tiwari was said to be drunk at the time of assault.

The incident came hot on the heels of the assault on Akhlaq, and not only united the Muslims and Dalits on a sociopolitical scale but also apprised the larger society with the grave danger the phenomenon of lynching presented. Soon after, there was Desh Bachao, Dwesh Mitao protest in many parts of Delhi and Uttar Pradesh. At Jantar Mantar in New Delhi, social leaders and activists belonging to different faiths and castes gathered to raise their voice against the lynching of Akhlaq and Chimma, two men unknown to each other, who had now become symbols of the unity of the exploited, the marginalized. Their common enemy were the upper caste Hindu men who were trying to impose their ideology on rest of the society. The dominant religion, and the dominant castes, were calling the shots. If Muslims were lynched on suspicion of cow slaughter, Dalits were lynched for trying to defy established social order by trying to enter a temple prohibited to them by the upper castes. Or, as the Una lynching case later proved, skinning cows which, the upper caste men alleged, they had slaughtered. Either way, the reasons for the assault were different but the consequences were the same. The men from the minority and Dalit communities paid with their life and self-respect in the upper caste Hindu men's pursuit of a traditional social order wherein they decided people's diet, their deities and their abodes. Post 2014, it was a revivalist era. Not many seem to remember that the Constitution of India had abolished untouchability through Article 17, and every Indian had the freedom to profess, practise and propagate any religion, and the State would not discriminate on the basis of religion, caste or gender. Society seemed paramount, the State, and the law, subservient to this street or mob trial.

File 3: The Mob Now Targets Dalits

However, Chimma could have been saved had the onlookers shown some courage. Or if they had read what Gautam Buddha, who denounced the Hindu caste system, had said about the lowest of the lows in the hierarchy. Buddha had cleared the picture by stating that one became Chandala not through birth but actions. In 2015 India, his words were not heeded. The subsequent years continued the abominable trend.

Every year on Eid-ul-Azha in New Delhi, towns of Uttar Pradesh, Rajasthan and Haryana, as Muslim men bring their goats to the butcher shop for sacrifice, it is common to find members of the Dalit community standing there in wait. It is the same at slaughterhouses where Muslims sacrifice buffaloes on Eid. As the animal is sacrificed, and a few minutes later skinned, the first *hissa* (share) is given to Dalit men present at the site. Some give it from the share meant for friends and relatives, some from the part meant for charity—every animal's meat is divided into three parts on Eid; one part stays with the family, the other two are equally distributed between friends and relatives, and the needy. Either way, the bond between Muslims and Dalits is strengthened afresh every year. Considering this a durable bond, if tacit, it was scarcely surprising that the Hindutva forces with their Muslim conquest post Akhlaq and others would go in for Dalits. The strategy was similar, if not identical: lay hands on lone Dalit men away from their comfort zone, accuse them of cow slaughter and proceed to lynch them. It was slightly more complicated than attacking a Muslim. The Dalits were also part of Hindu faith, making it impossible to stoke communal fire and reap

Una
The Lynchings and the Dalit Uprising
11 July 2016

political benefit. Although regarded inferior to the *dwija*, they could not be accused of their *pitrabhoomi* and *punyabhoomi* being in two separate countries. They were as much Indian as any twice born man or woman. Also, unlike Muslims, they had political parties catering specially to their interests. The Muslim community was rudderless, leaderless and directionless. The Dalits had people ready to step forward to hold their hand. Yet living a marginalized life with economic and educational enfeeblement, they identified with Muslims more than Brahmins. Inevitably, the rampant Hindutva forces went for them.

It started with low-key, localized operations in Kanpur and Aligarh in Uttar Pradesh where some Dalit men were attacked on suspicion of cow slaughter, thrashed and let go. These attacks happened in the early years of the new political dispensation at the Centre. Some thought these attacks to be a spillover of the attacks on Muslims alleged to be cow killers. The similarity between the plights of the communities began to be stark.

Then came Una, an assault so brazen and so belligerent that the nation's conscience was shaken. Here was a case of men drunk on caste system with all its inequities, impervious of the law of the land and arrogant due to the perceived support of their political masters. They grabbed four young men in their 20s, stripped them to their waist, tied them to a jeep and proceeded to give them a public lashing, whose echo could be felt far and wide. With belts, rods, hockey sticks and tubes of tyres, they treated the helpless men worse than slaves in the ancient days gone by. They were not merely thrashing the men they accused of cow slaughter but issuing a statement: Post 2014, Dalits were supposed to be at the mercy of upper castes. Their life and livelihood were secure on the goodwill of the upper castes. Any deviation, any defiance or any failure to comply with the command would result in public humiliation, even death. In living memory, it was the most gruesome public spectacle of caste-based assault: The unfortunate incident happened on 11 July 2016 when four Dalit youths were slapped, kicked and beaten up outside Mota Samadhiyala village, as they were skinning a dead cow brought from Bediya village. The victims were identified as Vashram Sarvaiya, his brother Ramesh and their cousins Ashok and Bechar, all residents of Mota Samadhiyala. The Sarvaiyas and others, however, still had to experience the worst. The members of BGRD took them to Una town nearby and again thrashed them with sticks and iron rods after tying them to a vehicle. Like in the case of Muslim men in Chittorgarh who were paraded naked, the Dalit men also paraded half-naked on the road in full public view. Again, as in the case of assaults on Muslim men, nobody came forward to their rescue. As in other attacks by right-wing forces, a video of the incident was promptly uploaded online. Yet again, the attackers felt confident enough of being able to defy the law, and strong enough to evoke a sense of fear among the victims and their community. Vashram later shared the details of the incident in his police complaint. He said that they had brought carcass from Bediya village.

> The accused came in a white car and asked us why we were slaughtering a cow. I told them that the cow was dead, and that we were only removing its skin. But they started abusing us and attacked us with iron pipes, sticks and a knife with which we were removing the skin of the carcass.[45]

---

[45] 'Gujarat: 7 of Dalit Family Beaten up for Skinning Dead Cow', *The Indian Express*, 20 July 2016.

 Lynch Files

The men beat up Vashram, along with Balu Sarvaiya's wife Kunvarben, his other son Ramesh and relatives Bechar Sarvaiya, Ashok Sarvaiya and Deveshi Sarvaiya. Later, the attackers took Vashram, Ramesh, Ashok and Bechar to Una, and proceeded to strip and flog them all the way to the police station. When the police arrived on the spot, the men fled in their vehicle. Nobody tried to stop them. It was reported after medical examination that Balu and Ramesh sustained head injuries, while others sustained injuries on other body parts due to attack by blunt objects.

In his complaint, Vashram named six persons—Pramodigiri Goswami, Balvant Balvant Dhiru, Rasik, Ramesh Jadav, Rakesh Joshi and Nagji Ahir. The last three were arrested. Vashram, Ramesh and Balu were also robbed of their mobile phones. Based on the complaint, five persons were booked under Section 307 (attempt to murder), Section 395 (loot) of the Indian Penal Code and the Scheduled Castes and the Scheduled Tribes (Prevention of Atrocities) Act. Three of them were later arrested.

The Una attack outraged the Dalit community in Gujarat and beyond, leading to widespread protests across the state in particular, and even in places like Mumbai, Chennai and Delhi later on. Incidentally, as in many cases related to Muslim dairy farmers or trader, a forensic report here too revealed that the cow skinned by the Dalits had been killed earlier by a lion. The Dalits were not guilty of killing the animal.

The Dalits though rebounded from the humiliation. Una proved to be a turning point in the long history of Dalit oppression. It became a badge of honour, the day the community turned the corner. They called upon the strength unique to the exploited, rallied around each other and proceeded to issue a statement of their own: The days of Manu Smriti, of which there were whispers of revival, were gone.

> The Dalits were here, defiant and independent. With a youth leader like Jignesh Mevani showing the way, they held a long march in Gujarat. Beginning early August, thousands of Dalits started a 10-day march from Ahmedabad to Una to protest the atrocities on the community in Gujarat.

Led by Mevani, the Azaadin Koon (March for Freedom) covered a distance of more than 300 kilometres. It ended on 15 August in Una, where the community members pledged independence from exploitation. And Dalits, many hard-pressed to earn their living for the day, left everything to join in. The community also presented 10 key demands before the government. It included providing them with alternative livelihood options, reservation for Dalits under the Reservation Act, allotment of land for Dalit families, strong legal framework to fight atrocities against Dalits, ensuring that people from the community do not work as manual scavengers and implementation of Forest Rights Act.

Some members then proceeded to dump cow carcasses at the secretariat, sending a strong signal that the community was not ready to take things lying down.

 Lynch Files

> The cow, as a living being, could be regarded as a mother by upper castes in some parts of the country. But cow, when dead, was not the responsibility of the Dalits. The slogan 'Your mother, you take care of it' reverberated across the state, as the community, which brings up 7 per cent of the electorate in Gujarat, punched above its weight. The Dalits stopped skinning dead cows and depositing their carcass away from the site of death, leaving the task to Brahmins, Kshatriyas and Vaisyas.

They stopped cleaning the manholes too. The traditional caste vocations were turned upside down. The society was shaken. The Dalit resistance had the desired result. Prime Minister Narendra Modi, who had maintained dubious silence when a number of Muslim dairy farmers and traders were dubbed smugglers and murdered by cow militia, was forced to speak. His statement, 'If you have a problem, if you feel like attacking someone, attack me, not my Dalit brothers. If you want to shoot anyone, shoot me, not my Dalit brothers,' came almost a month after the Una tragedy, clearly in response to the long march of Mevani and company. The statement seemed high on histrionics—his strength—and low on sincerity—his obvious weakness. However, coming as it did from the prime minister of the country, it stopped cow militia in its tracks. The number of attacks on Dalits came down drastically. The Muslims had to bear the brunt.

File 4
Lynched and Forgotten!

WHEN TRAGEDIES WERE DISMISSED

10 States and Many More Lynchings

There were incidents which made headlines. From Dadri and Una to Alwar and Hapur, many of these incidents caught the eye of the media. That helped generate greater awareness and accountability. Questions were asked of the police, of the *gau rakshaks* and even of the victims' families. At the other end were incidents which failed to get the attention they deserved. The media also either stayed ignorant or even when the incident came to light it was dismissed without sustained enquiry and investigation. That only compounded the tragedy. The men and women, who lost their lives in such assaults, or escaped with injuries, deserved attention. Ranging from a Dalit couple in Rajkot to Muslim boys in Dadri (yet again), each of the stories was sorrowful and pointed to a lapse in security. The most notable though was the dragging out of a man from jail and his lynching by a mob in Dimapur. Even considering that he was a rape accused, he deserved to be treated according to the law of our land. The mob giving out instant justice is not the way our Constitution makers had planned.

Here is a lowdown to some of the incidents that largely escaped the attention of our society and polity.

Dimapur Lynching

This March 2015 case made headlines in most Northeast cities, but not in the Hindi heartland or the southern states. A mob of about 7,000–10,000 people broke into the Central Jail at Dimapur in Nagaland and dragged out a man accused of rape.

The mob paraded him naked and beat him to death. The police watched the parade.

Three Boys Lynched

This lynching incident in Dadri happened a little before the better-known case of Akhlaq. And if the local authorities had taken corrective action, maybe subsequent lynchings could have been averted. Here three Muslim boys, Anas, Arif and Nazim, were lynched for carrying buffaloes in their truck by alleged animal rights activists on 2 August 2015 in Dadri's Kaimrala village in Uttar Pradesh. The boys were considered as cattle thieves. The police filed a case against the victims for being cattle thieves, but no case was filed against the mob for murder!

Singh Lynched in Delhi

The nation's capital reported a lynching case from near the gate of a Metro station in East Delhi. It was a particularly sad case as the victim was punished for upholding the law. In May 2017, an e-rickshaw driver Ravinder Singh was lynched by 15–20 youths. Ravinder Singh had earlier in the day stopped one of the accused from urinating in public. Venkaiah Naidu, then a Union minister, praised Singh for promoting Swachh Bharat Abhiyan.

 Lynch Files

Lynching of Zafar Khan

In June 2017, another case of a man being punished for positive work was reported. Zafar Khan, an activist in Rajasthan, was allegedly killed by some municipal officials at Pratapgarh district for objecting to clicking photographs of women relieving themselves in open. The civic body workers were said to be out to promote Swachh Bharat campaign.

Men Made to Eat Cow Dung

They were close to the national capital, but it did not dissuade BGRD activists from laying their hands on two Muslim men, Mukhtar and Rizwan, who were transporting beef to Delhi by a car in June 2016. Dubbed cow traffickers, the men were stopped at K M Payal Expressway in Haryana by some *gau rakshaks* and manhandled. Their life was spared after they were force-fed cow dung and urine mixed with curd and ghee. The cow vigilantes later released a video online where the two were shown sitting on the highway, their faces swollen, and eating cow refuse and vomiting. The video was almost unanimously condemned.

Man Attacked on Eid in Haryana

In August 2018, Yamin Khokhar, a resident of Rohtak in Haryana, was attacked by a mob on Eid-ul-Azha on suspicion of beating a calf to slaughter it on Eid. According to a resident, Yamin had hit the calf in self-defence after the animal had struck his daughter. After some time, the calf died, and the mob alleged that he had hit the calf to slaughter it later on Eid. It did not strike anybody that only an adult, healthy animal can be slaughtered on Eid, not an animal yet to come of age or lame.

The mob attacked Yamin's house, forcing the family to flee. The police arrested Yamin and his brother Yaseen, even as the mob buried the carcass of the animal in the local Muslim cemetery. Nobody among the attackers was arrested.

DSP Lynched in Srinagar

Irate mob outside Jama Masjid in Srinagar lynched senior police officer, DSP Ayub Pandit in June 2017. The incident happened during the last days of Ramzan when the faithful seek spiritual elevation. Pandit though had no such luck. Posted at the mosque, he was doing his duty manning the access control at the place. Around 12.30 am, he was attacked by a mob which stripped him naked and stoned him to death. However, the officer, in his defence, had earlier fired from his pistol in which three persons were injured. The mob later went on the rampage in the area.

Truck Attacked in Udhampur

In October 2015, alleged Hindutva extremists attacked a truck in Udhampur with petrol bombs, following rumours that the truck was carrying dead cows. It was assumed that the cows had been killed by the driver and his aides on the truck. The driver of the truck, Zahid Ahmed Bhat, was actually carrying cow carcasses. At the time he was attacked by cow militia, he was actually resting. Zahid succumbed to his injuries 10 days later, sparking off violence in the state. The mob took to the streets in Anantnag and blocked the Jammu–Srinagar highway by burning tyres. The people shouted slogans and pelted stones before being forced to disperse. Later, it emerged from a forensic laboratory report that the cows had died due to food poisoning, and they had not been slaughtered. Zahid ended up a victim of the mob's misplaced anger.

Lynching in Nagaon, Assam

Two Muslim men, Abu Hanifa and Riyazuddin Ali, were brutally killed for alleged theft of cows for slaughter in Nagaon district of Assam on 30 April 2017. Ali used to drive a shared tempo and Hanifa was a vegetable vendor. On the fatal day, the two had stepped out of Hanifa's house together. Some three hours later, Ali's family got a call that Ali and his friends were accused of cow theft and being thrashed by a mob. By the time the family members could reach them at the hospital, they had died, leaving many questions behind. Abu Hanifa and Riyazuddin Ali were finally buried together. As in life, they remained together after death.

The case was very similar to some of the incidents in Jharkhand and Rajasthan.

Muslim Couple Attacked

Madhya Pradesh reported a number of small-scale instances of cow-related violence. In January 2016, a Muslim couple was attacked at Khirkiya railway station in the Harda district of the state by cow protection goons over allegations that they were carrying beef. Here too, the police instead of first arresting the men who attacked the couple took the meat they were carrying in a bag in their possession and sent to laboratory for examination. There, it was discovered that it was not cow meat but buffalo meat. The police registered a case against two Gau Raksha Samiti activists for causing hurt and criminal intimidation. They were arrested. Yet the lingering feeling was the police's first attention to the meat rather than human beings being attacked.

Teenager Slaps a 45-Year-Old Man

In February 2018, a video showing a teenage boy Vijay Meena slapping a 45-year-old man in Jaipur went viral. In the video, Meena was seen forcing the man to say Jai Shri Ram. He slapped him around 25 times to make him say Jai Shri Ram. The man answered, 'Parvardigaar sabse bada hai' (God is the greatest). Later, a complaint was lodged at Jaipur's Abu Road city police station. Meena was arrested for voluntarily causing hurt, promoting enmity and hurting religious sentiments.

Muslim Women Beaten Up in Madhya Pradesh

On 26 July 2016, two burqa-clad Muslim women were allegedly beaten up at Mandsaur railway station by the Bajrang Dal members, on the suspicion of carrying beef. The women were attacked on the bus, forced to alight and subjected to communal abuse. On examination, it was found that the meat they were carrying was buffalo meat. Later, speaking to news agencies, the women stated, 'When we were coming to Mandsaur, some Bajrang Dal activists stopped us and inquired about what were we carrying. We told them that it was *"Paade ke meat"* (buffalo calf meat). They did not listen to us and said that it was beef.'

The men were arrested under Sections 341, 323 and 34 of the Indian Penal Code. The sections pertain to punishment for wrongful restraint, voluntarily causing hurt and acts done by several persons in furtherance of common intention, respectively.

Attack in Bengal

The menace of cow lynching made its abominable presence felt in August 2017 in Bengal. In this case, three young men, Nazrul Islam (25), Anwar Hussain (19) and Hafizul Sheikh (19), were transporting cattle from the Dhupguri cattle market to Tufanganj in Cooch Behar, Northeast Bengal. On the journey, they were waylaid by a mob near Barohalia village in Jalpaiguri. The attack initially did not make media headlines until *IndiaSpend* gave space to it in September 2017.

The three men were coming back after purchasing seven cattle from a market. They had lost their way to Tufanganj in the darkness of the night. It is here that they were noticed by locals. Finding that they were travelling with cattle, the mob questioned them for more than an hour and demanded ₹50,000 from them to allow them safe passage. The men had no money to buy peace. Nazrul, who was driving the vehicle, managed to escape. His two fellow travellers paid with their life. The villagers tried to set the truck on fire too. The case gave credence to the lingering feeling that many of the cow militia attacks were a ruse to make money rather than protect the cow.

Mangalore Case

A Muslim man was stripped, tied to a pole and beaten up by a mob in Mangalore in Karnataka. His crime? Speaking to his Hindu colleague! 'We have arrested 13 persons.... Some of them are members of Bajrang Dal,' said S. Murugan, the Mangalore police commissioner. The 29-year-old man was in his car with the woman one evening when he was surrounded and attacked by a mob. Speaking to a woman from another religion was considered a crime by the mob in one of the major cities of India!

Killed Due to Muslim Company

In November 2015, Harish Poojari, a school dropout, met with a gruesome end. In the evening of 12 November 2015, he had stepped out to buy milk for the tea his mother was preparing and never returned. Instead, next morning his body arrived at his residence with marks of savage beating. The family could not understand the reason. He had no animosity with any local elements. It turned out that on the fateful day he had accompanied his Muslim friend Samiullah. In fact, he was walking to the shop when Samiullah, who was on his bike, offered to drop him home. On the way, a group of men from Bajrang Dal attacked them with knives. Samiullah survived, Harish could not. He had been attacked 14 times and his intestines were pulled out! He was attacked on the mere suspicion of being a Muslim because he was in the company of one! The local police later arrested four Bajrang Dal volunteers.

Andhra Lynching

In August 2016, two men belonging to the lower caste were attacked by cow vigilantes in Andhra Pradesh. It was reported by NDTV that Mokati Elisa and his brother Lazar were hired to skin a cow that had died of electrocution. Much like in the Una case, while they were on the job, the brothers were attacked by around 100 *gau rakshaks* who arrived at the spot accusing them of stealing and killing the animal.

Assam Savagery

On 8 June 2018, two boys—Nilotpal Das (29) and Abhijeet Nath (30)—who had gone to visit the Kangthilangso waterfall in Karbi Anglong were killed on their way back. Their vehicle was stopped at Panjuri by some villagers, who pulled them out and killed them on the suspicion that they were child-lifters.

This happened due to a rumour on WhatsApp and social media. A legal case has been initiated for the incident. It was a rare case when the upper caste men were at the receiving end of the misplaced ire of the local community.

Dalit ManCed in Rajkot

It was among a handful of incidents of lynching of Dalit men after the aggressive response of the community to Una lynching. In this case, a 40-year-old Dalit man, Mukesh Vaniya, was allegedly lynched in Rajkot district. According to his wife, the employees from a local factory asked them their caste. When it was confirmed that they were Dalits, the employees wanted the couple to pick up garbage. When Vaniya and his wife refused, they were beaten.

It did not end there. Vaniya was picked up, tied to a pole and assaulted brutally with metal rods for more than an hour. He died. A video was made of the torture inflicted on the Dalit man and was widely circulated in social media. Our news media failed to give the incident the space it deserved.

Beaten to Death in Uttar Pradesh

A 22-year-old Dalit man was beaten to death by five people who suspected him of stealing in Baghra village.

The victim was called Ankit. Among his attackers were Rampal, Lokesh, Ajay, Amit and Haseen. The five accused suspected Ankit, a labourer, of stealing goods. Ankit was rushed to a hospital where he was declared brought dead.

On the basis of a complaint by the labourer's mother, a case was registered against the five men under relevant sections of India Penal Code and the Scheduled Castes and the Scheduled Tribes (Prevention of Atrocities) Act. Shortly after, the five men were arrested. They confessed their crime.

Karnataka Killing over Beef

On 17 June 2016, some 40 members of Bajrang Dal brutally attacked a Dalit family in Koppa, Karnataka, for allegedly possessing beef. According to a media report, the head of the family suffered a fracture, while other family members escaped with minor injuries. Their crime? Storing beef! They could count themselves lucky, considering Akhlaq had to pay with his life for a similar allegation in Dadri.

The local police filed a case against the attackers under the Scheduled Castes and the Scheduled Tribes (Prevention of Atrocities) Amendment Act, 2015.

Dalit Boys in Chittorgarh

In April 2016, three Dalit boys, all teenagers, were paraded naked in Rajasthan's Bassi Tehsil on suspicion of stealing a bike. The boys were allegedly caught by a mob and then stripped in public, before being paraded around the district. The boys belonged to Kanjay community and later confessed to their crime.

Bidar Lynching

A 32-year-old man, Mohammed Azam, was lynched to death in Bidar on rumours of child-lifting in July 2018. A techie based in Hyderabad, Azam had gone on a picnic with his friends.

The men offered chocolates to children in Bootakula village along the way. The villagers doubted their credentials and tried to stop them. On failing to do so, the residents of Murki pounced upon the men in the car. The police tried to come to the rescue of the accused and arrested 28 people. While the lives of Azam's friends, including a Qatar resident, were saved, he ended up paying with his own life.

Dhule Violence

On 1 July 2018, five people from nomadic tribal communities were lynched on allegation of being child-lifters. They were lynched at Rainpada in Dhule, Maharashtra. According to the police, local residents first interrogated the five people after they spotted them offering biscuits to a local girl. As rumours of child-lifters being around spread in the area—much like cow smugglers—the victims were caught, physically attacked and then dragged through a 400 metre stretch. They died later due to physical violence.

Cop Attacked in Latur

In this case, the tables turned. The mob laid its hands on a policeman, forcing him to do its bidding. It so happened that on 19 February 2016, an assistant sub-inspector Yunus Sheikh and his colleague K. Awaskar prevented around 25 youth of the little known Shivaji Jayanti Mandal from hoisting a saffron flag at the Ambedkar Chowk in Latur, Maharashtra.

The next day, a mob of around a hundred laid siege to the police station and forced Sheikh to come out. The mob then made him hold a saffron flag and chant 'Jai Bhawani' slogans as he marched across the township in utter humiliation. His Hindu colleague was spared the onslaught.

Dalit Man Dead in Kanpur

In August 2016, a Dalit man died allegedly due to beating with rods at a police outpost in Uttar Pradesh's Kanpur district. He was allegedly humiliated, abused and thrashed over allegations of robbery. Earlier, he was attacked by a mob before being handed over to the police.

Later, his brother alleged that Kamal and he were kicked around like football in the lock-up. The police tried to get a confession from the brothers. A little later, Kamal was found hanging and Nirmal was allowed to go home. All the 15 policemen at the outpost were immediately suspended.

Man Lynched in Palwal

In August 2018, there was yet another instance of lynching not too far from the NCR. This time in Palwal. The incident took place on the outskirts of Behraula village. According to a family, three thieves tried to steal their cattle at night. They were woken up, as were other villagers due to the chaos, and they managed to catch one of the alleged thieves while the other two escaped. However, instead of handing over the alleged thief to the police, they beat the man to death.

The police registered an FIR and arrested one man for the attack.

Ramgarh Yet Again

This case happened days after Eid celebrations in June 2018, and roughly around the Hapur lynching tragedy. In Ramgarh, yet again, a Muslim man, Touheed Ansari, was lynched by a mob. In this instance, Ansari was riding on a bike to purchase groceries for his guests when he met with an accident. In that accident, the meat that he was carrying also fell on the road. The mob took it for beef and attacked Ansari who tried to run away from the spot. Later, his brutalized body was recovered from the railway track. It manifests clear signs of deep and sustained torture. The police confiscated his bike.

Ansaris Killed before Eid in Jharkhand

This case made news for a brief while just before Eid-ul-Fitr celebrations in June 2018. This time, in Jharkhand's Godda district, a mob allegedly lynched two men over suspicion of stealing their cattle. According to the police, residents of tribal-dominated Dullu village caught hold of the two victims—Sirabuddin Ansari (35) and Murtaza Ansari (30)—and accused them of stealing 13 buffaloes from one Munshi Murmu and others on the night of 12 June. The two victims were residents of Taljhari in the district, about 200 kilometres from Ranchi. The accused villagers, after killing the duo, brought back their bodies to Dullu village on bicycles. The police arrested two of the men accused of killing the Ansaris.

Assaulted in Kerala

Lynching in the name of the cow was least likely to take place in Kerala, considering beef is part of everyday diet in the state. But on 28 June 2018, an incident was reported from Kollam where Jalal, a cattle trader, was attacked by two persons while returning from cattle market in Charummoodu. Jalal was accompanied by his relative Jaleel and driver Sabu when they were waylaid at the Muslim street by the attackers who wielded hockey sticks and canes. The three were badly injured. According to Jalal, 'When we reached Muslim street they stopped our vehicle and started arguing about where were we taking the cattle and started manhandling us.' Jalal was taking the cattle to sell in his hometown when he was attacked allegedly by RSS men. The police arrested two RSS workers, Vishnu and Gopakumar, in this regard and charged them with an attempt to murder.

File 5
Aftermath

SUPREME COURT SHOWS THE WAY

If Right to Life activists were looking for a lifeline, it came their way on 17 July 2018 with the honourable Supreme Court's three-bench judgment in the Tehseen Poonawala versus the Union of India case. Taking a serious view of the spate of lynchings India has seen since 2014—and there has been an increase each passing year—the apex court not only provided punitive action but also gave preventive and remedial measures. And the media, clearly exhausted with the pattern of lynchings, latched on to every word and interpretation of the judgment with absolute seriousness. Hailing the judgment, *The Hindu*'s editorial said,

> In its 45-page order, the Supreme Court has significantly located lynching and vigilante violence in a socio-political framework linked to disrespect for an inclusive social order, rising intolerance and growing polarisation. There is an implicit indictment of the preponderant mood of the times when it says that 'hate crimes as a product of intolerance, ideological dominance and prejudice ought not to be tolerated'.[46]

---

[46] 'Lynching and the Law', *The Hindu*, 19 July 2018.

The Indian Express observed, 'Supreme Court has broken the silence on lynching. It must be heard in letter and spirit.' Hailing the judgment, it said,

> The silence broken by the court is of the political class—most unforgivably, of government which has so far failed to acknowledge the gravity of the crime.... The court must be applauded, therefore, for the unambiguous way in which it has expressed its revulsion at 'horrendous acts of mobocracy' and forthrightly warned against these patterns of violence becoming 'the new normal'.[47]

Hindustan Times highlighted the Supreme Court's 11-point prescription which included 'a slew of directions, including preventive, remedial and punitive steps to deal with the crime'.

The Urdu press was even more enthusiastic in welcoming the judgment. Newspapers such as *Rashtriya Sahara*, *The Inquilaab*, *Dawat* and *Akhbar-e-Nau* opened their pages with the news of the judgment. To them, the judgment was a tool to control the hitherto untamed, unrestrained and unhindered growth of non-stage actors like cow militia. In their wording, the editorials exhibited fresh hope that the worst may be behind us after the court judgment. Clearly, Chief Justice Dipak Misra's judgment had come as a balm for a society struggling to come to terms with the inhuman reality of lynching. The judgment offered both hope and solution.

It said,

> No individual in his own capacity or as a part of a group, which within no time assumes the character of a mob,

---

[47] 'The Silence Broken by the Court is of the Political Class...', *The Indian Express*, available at: https://indianexpress.com/article/opinion/editorials/the-new-abnormal-supreme-court-mob-lynching-5263734/.

can take law into his/their hands and deal with a person treating him as guilty. That is not only contrary to the paradigm of established legal principles in our legal system but also inconceivable in a civilized society that respects the fundamental tenets of the rule of law.[48]

In a wide-ranging 45-page judgment, the apex court brought to attention instances of lynching in the United States and also recalled a judgment in the case of khap panchayats not so far back in time. Condemning mob violence against the minorities and Dalits as 'horrendous acts of mobocracy', the court asked Parliament to pass a law, establishing lynching as a separate offence with punishment. The three-judge bench—including Justice A. M. Khanwilkar and Justice D. Y. Chandrachud besides the Chief Justice—held that it was the obligation of the State to ensure the safety of all citizens and make sure that the 'pluralistic social fabric' of the country holds against mob violence. The judges also held that the new law should be strong enough to instil fear in the minds of the perpetrators of violence.

The honourable court stated,

> Lynching, at one point of time, was so rampant in the United States that Mark Twain had observed in his inimitable style that it had become 'the United States of Lyncherdom'.... In this context, we may reproduce a passage from Shakti Vahini (supra) which, though pronounced in a different context, has certain significance:- 'The "Khap Panchayats" or such assembly should not take the law into their hands and further cannot assume the character of the law implementing agency, for that authority has not been conferred upon

---

[48] Supreme Court's Tehseen Poonawala versus the Union of India judgment.

them under any law. Law has to be allowed to sustain by the law enforcement agencies. For example, when a crime under Indian Penal Code is committed, an assembly of people cannot impose the punishment. They have no authority. They are entitled to lodge an FIR or inform the police. They may also facilitate so that the Accused is dealt with in accordance with law. But, by putting forth a stand that they are spreading awareness, they really can neither affect others' fundamental rights nor cover up their own illegal acts. It is simply not permissible. In fact, it has to be condemned as an act abhorrent to law and, therefore, it has to stop. Their activities are to be stopped in entirety'.[49]

The apex court did not shy away from pointing the silence of the bystanders, the people who stand and watch a man being murdered before their eyes in public domain.

> Lynching is an affront to the rule of law and to the exalted values of the Constitution itself. We may say without any fear of contradiction that lynching by unruly mobs and barbaric violence arising out of incitement and instigation cannot be allowed to become the order of the day. Such vigilantism, be it for whatever purpose or borne out of whatever cause, has the effect of undermining the legal and formal institutions of the State and altering the constitutional order. These extrajudicial attempts under the guise of protection of the law have to be nipped in the bud; lest it would lead to rise of anarchy and lawlessness which would plague and corrode the nation like an epidemic. The tumultuous dark clouds of vigilantism have the effect of shrouding the glorious ways of democracy and

---

[49] Supreme Court's Tehseen Poonawala versus the Union of India judgment.

justice leading to tragic breakdown of the law and transgressing all forms of civility and humanity. Unless these incidents are controlled, the day is not far when such monstrosity in the name of self-professed morality is likely to assume the shape of a huge cataclysm.... Rising intolerance and growing polarisation expressed through spate of incidents of mob violence cannot be permitted to become the normal way of life or the normal state of law and order in the country.... Hate crimes as a product of intolerance, ideological dominance and prejudice ought not to be tolerated; lest it results in a reign of terror. Extra judicial elements and non-State actors cannot be allowed to take the place of law or the law enforcing agency.... Plurality of voices celebrates the constitutionalist idea of a liberal democracy and ought not to be suppressed. That is the idea and essence of our nation which cannot be, to borrow a line from Rabindranath Tagore, 'broken up into fragments by narrow domestic walls' of caste, creed, race, class or religion. Pluralism and tolerance are essential virtues and constitute the building blocks of a truly free and democratic society.... Lynching and mob violence are creeping threats that may gradually take the shape of a Typhon-like monster as evidenced in the wake of the rising wave of incidents of recurring patterns by frenzied mobs across the country instigated by intolerance and misinformed by circulation of fake news and false stories. There has been an unfortunate litany of spiralling mob violence and agonized horror presenting a grim and gruesome picture that compels us to reflect whether the populace of a great Republic like ours has lost the values of tolerance to sustain a diverse culture. Besides, bystander apathy, numbness of the mute spectators of the scene of the crime, inertia of the law enforcing machinery to prevent such crimes and nip them in the bud and grandstanding of the incident by the perpetrators of the crimes including in the social media aggravates the entire problem. One must constantly remind oneself that an attitude of morbid intolerance is absolutely intolerable and agonizingly painful.[50]

The court's strong words forced Prime Minister Narendra Modi to finally express himself unambiguously on the subject. He said, 'I want to make it clear, lynching is a crime, whatever the motive.'

Not everybody was convinced. And pointed out that the honourable court had earlier instructed nodal officers to be appointed to prevent such crimes. But the violence continued. As reported by *The Hindu*,

> The judgment came in a contempt petition filed by activist Tehseen Poonawalla. It said that despite the Supreme Court order to the States to prevent lynchings and violence by cow vigilantes, the crime continued with impunity. 'Despite your order to the States to appoint nodal officers to prevent such incidents, there was a lynching and death just 60 km away from Delhi just recently,' senior advocate Indira Jaising had submitted. Ms Jaising argued that the incidents of lynchings go 'beyond the description of law and order ... these crimes have a pattern and a motive. For instance, all these instances happen on highways. This court had asked the States to patrol the highways'.[51]

---

[50] Supreme Court's Tehseen Poonawala versus the Union of India judgment.
[51] 'SC asks Parliament to Bring in Special Law against Lynching', available at: https://www.thehindu.com/news/national/sc-judgment-condemns-recent-incidents-of-lynching/article24440041.ece *The Hindu*, 17 July 2018.

Some legal experts were not convinced of the need for a fresh law, arguing that what was needed was political will to implement the existing laws. 'We already have laws to tackle mob violence or attempts to disrupt communal harmony. We need no stringent laws but strong political will to control the menace,' they argued. Others believed that a special law will do away with any ambiguity with the subject. Among those voicing their assent were former Attorney General Mukul Rohatgi and senior advocate Ajit Kumar Sinha who said that the specific law and order issue like lynching which has affected India's international image has to be tackled with a 'special' and 'deterrent' law.

The need for a stringent law was felt within four days of the Supreme Court judgment when the entire game of alleged complicity of the police and *gau rakshaks* came to the fore in the Rakbar lynching. He was badly mauled by cow vigilante groups in Alwar. However, he died in police custody. It gave rise to a game of passing the buck. Did the victim die at the hands of the so-called *gau rakshaks*? Or did police hit him when he was in their custody, leading to his death? And was he allowed to die to avoid uncomfortable revelations later on. These questions were openly aired after the tragedy. Only time will tell the answer, but, yes, if a law dealing with lynching were in place, the answers could have been easier to find.

Similarly, more than a couple of weeks after the judgment, the widow of Alimuddin was still waiting for her husband's death certificate. Soon the court gave her room for optimism when on 13 August 2018, during a hearing of Samiuddin's petition, the court directed the Meerut police to give security cover to Samiuddin, lone lynching survivor in the assault in which Qasim was killed and Samiuddin seriously injured.

The Supreme Court judgment has given hope that dawn may not be an illusion.

DESECRATING HATE, BIGOTRY AND EVERYTHING THAT LEADS TO LYNCHING

As it turned out...

> A man was killed after being dragged out of his bedroom. A boy was killed boarding a train. Another man was pulled out of a truck on the highway. And a man was lynched walking his cows home. The message was clear:
>
> 'Wherever you may go,
> the cow vigilantes will get you.'

The state will stand and nod, invariably book the victims, even file FIRs against the dead, while the *gau rakshaks*, often impervious to law, are regarded as part of the long, invisible arm of the law themselves.

A little under five years after the right-wing BJP got a majority to form a government on its own at the Centre, lynching of the innocent is the new normal. A nation that reacted with outrage when Akhlaq was brutalized has become accustomed to repeat performances, with each new killing attracting less and less of criticism; it is like it has seeped into our culture. Often our media treats a lynching incident with the indifference reserved for a local pickpocket or bootlegger nabbed by the police. In some quarters, there is cynicism too: 'It is wrong, it should not be done, but they asked for it. Why do they insist on killing cows?' With such thoughts aired freely in drawing room discussions, our insensitivity has touched a new high. And after cricket, the humble cow is the biggest unifying or dividing force in the country today. Increasingly, it seems that the state seems to care more for the cows than human beings. In a gesture which reminded one of the words of *a gau rakshak* who claimed after a lynching incident in Rajasthan, 'In the cow reside 33 crore deities. We will not let them kill the cow. We will kill for the cow,' the Rajasthan and Haryana governments competed to be the most bovine friendly states. Rajasthan, in fact, introduced a 10 per cent cow protection surcharge on the stamp duty for non-judicial instruments. Haryana, meanwhile, decided to set up a cow protection task force and increased the fund for bovine welfare while cutting down on allocation for education. Also, the Haryana government came up with the Gauvansh Sanrakshan and Gausamvardhan Act, 2015, which besides making cow slaughter and smuggling punishable with up to 10 years in jail made it practically impossible to buy cattle independent of animal markets. A buyer had to procure five copies of proof of the deed and submit the certificates to the local revenue office, veterinary doctor, etc. In a country notorious for bureaucratic red-tapism, it practically shut the door on procurement of even aged cows, leaving the poor dairy farmers susceptible to both fake accusations and real lynchings. Not surprisingly, the states have registered numerous instances of lynching, and an ever-increasing number of FIRs and arrests, for alleged cow smuggling. In both the states, as indeed Jharkhand, the political bosses refrained from explicitly criticising those responsible for lynching or visiting the bereaved families, or even enabling them to start life all over again with some financial aid. Instead, the police almost regularly filed countercharges against the affected, accusing them of cow slaughter while filing complaints against the *gau rakshaks* in comparatively milder terms. As a result, more than four years since the first instance in Pune, no *gau rakshak* has had a final punishment pronounced. Many were in fact able to get bail within a few days of arrest; in one case, an accused stepped out of the jail to a hero's welcome on the same day as the man who had been badly mauled by *gau rakshaks* was discharged from the hospital.

Over a period of time, some of the affected persons might come to terms with the grievous loss, but the road back will be long, lonely and challenging. For proof, one only has to visit the age-old house of Akhlaq in Dadri. Around three years after Akhlaq was murdered in September 2015, his house wore a deserted look on Eid-ul-Azha in August 2018. Incidentally, this was the festival on which he was fatally accused of cow slaughter. Instead, in 2018, the entrance to his locked house was marked by a cow dung cake. Across the lane was another heap of cow dung cakes. Maybe it was unintentional, and the locals had just used an unused house out of convenience, but the presence of cow refuse near the doorstep of the man killed on suspicion of cow slaughter spoke a million words about dominant religion crushing all before it. As for Akhlaq's family, it has been more than three years since they left the premises; the brothers, who were once close together, now live in separate dwellings. And no, they have not been able to sacrifice any animal on Eid, a requirement for men of faith who have the means. It goes against Article 25 of the Constitution, but we are living in times when street mob

 Lynch Files

decides not just your right to practise your faith but even your right to life.

If there was any consolation for Akhlaq's family, it was that they were in it together with other victims of lynching. On Eid-ul-Azha in 2018, Qasim's son wore a dazed expression while Samiuddin had tears constantly streaming out of his eyes. Both Qasim and Samiuddin were attacked not too far from Dadri soon after Eid-ul-Fitr in June 2018, giving rise to suspicion that all the actions had political blessings. In far away Jharkhand, Alimuddin Ansari's widow Mariam kept her tears in check as she sought to lay hands on his death certificate which would enable her to use her late husband's savings for her children. As for Rakbar, when Jamaat-e-Islami volunteers went a day ahead of Eid to extend a token of help, the family did not even know that Eid was a few hours away. The month since Rakbar was lynched in July 2018 had gone in coming to terms with the loss, and gearing up to fight one more round, knowing the local police could yet impose some punitive clause on the deceased, or even arrest Aslam, the sole survivor of cow vigilante attack that took the life of Rakbar.

Where the victims' family cut a sorry figure, the attackers complained that 'innocent men' had been framed by the police! In Alwar, it was not unusual to hear that the police had failed to nab the real culprits, and those in jail were innocent! Worse, a *gau rakshak* leader complained that they stepped in because the police was hindered by law! Clearly, the days of circumventing the law are in for *gau rakshaks*.

No wonder, they feel emboldened to not just lynch men to death but also record their deed for wider consumption, almost like a victory shield. The way things have panned out since 2014, lynchings have become a command performance with an assumed silent but receptive audience, and a sure adversary. The films uploaded online work through the fear factor, a policy of relentless intimidation of the Other—this time not through assault on the women, as has been the case since time immemorial, but through graphic violence inflicted on the helpless men, supposedly the custodians of the fairer sex in traditional society. It is a weapon of choice far more effective than public shooting, riots or staged encounters. The state does not sully its hands; the non-state actors do the job. They talk of assumed majority suffering and stoke it further.

It is but this feeling of being above the law that has resulted in our democracy descending to the realms of mobocracy. It is in such a society that a man as widely respected as Swami Agnivesh was assaulted twice in the span of a few weeks in the summer of 2018, once outside the office of the ruling BJP! It reminded of some of similar lynching instances in the United States in the nineteenth century, or Pakistan in the twenty-first century. In fact, like the serious attacks on Agnivesh, Pakistan too recorded the fatal attack on Salman Taseer, a man who spoke up for the minorities in that country.

> Simply put, Indian mobocracy operates on the simple principle of 'my way or the highway'. Anybody deemed to be opposed to Hindutva thugs is either disposed off in the name of cow slaughter or sought to be intimidated into silence, like in the case of Agnivesh.

The lynchings buy the silence of the aggrieved community, the assault aims at silencing activists and liberals alike. Either way,

 Lynch Files

the space for dialogue, debate and dissent shrinks further. And India stands on the brink of an authoritarian power structure which muzzles as it pleases.

It has already taken its toll. Not only have we had repeated instances of lynching of Muslims and Dalits, we have seen some of the worst caste-based discrimination since Independence. We had a man burnt to death for daring to step into an upper caste temple, an old woman forced to carry her slippers on her head in Uttar Pradesh merely because she had committed the folly of walking with her slippers while passing in front of a Thakur's house, and an old man forced to lick the spit of an upper caste man because he had dared to walk while Thakur Sahab had stepped out of his house. All this happened in Uttar Pradesh where supposedly a saint calls the shots. The things were not much better in Gujarat or Rajasthan where instances were reported of a lower caste groom being forced to get down from his horse on the day of the wedding, or a marriage party of Dalits refused permission by upper castes to use a well in their village. Inevitably, this death and discrimination has brought the minorities and Dalits together.

Someday, if all the Muslim and Dalit men lynched in the name of cow slaughter, cattle theft or child lifting were to be buried together in a common cemetery, it would be like a miniature replica of Kohima War Cemetery. Each tombstone would have a story to tell, each narrator would have a tear to shed. Among the most tragic would be the stories of four Muslim men, Naeem, Siraj, Sajju and Sheikh Haleem, who were lynched near Jamshedpur in May 2017 merely because the locals gave credence to rumours spread through WhatsApp. The messages warned the locals about the presence of a child-lifting gang in their city. Not inclined to cross-check a piece of information spread through dubious means, the locals took the message for final truth. Result? Lynching of four men who were out as part of their professional needs. The same evening, three Hindu men, Uttam Verma, Vikas and Gangesh Gupta, were lynched by tribal men on similar rumours of child-lifting. If ever WhatsApp messages had a devastating impact, it was in Jamshedpur on that fateful day.

There will be a prominent epitaph for Akhlaq too, and a little note for victims of Una who were struck with belts and canes in full public view for skinning a dead cow. There will be a remembrance note for Abdul Shameer too, who was caught while driving a tempo with ageing cattle to Mangalore. Total strangers attacked him merely on assumption of cow slaughter, as did an autorickshaw driver whom he knew. Strangers and acquaintances alike united to attack a man who was not even given a chance to defend himself. Cow protection was supreme, justice could wait. Although his skull was hit with a trident, Shameer survived, just about, needing the generosity of the larger secular society to cope with astronomical medical bills. The state—ruled by Congress this time—yet again kept a distance. Just as it did in Jamshedpur where the government thought it fit to offer a compensation of a measly ₹2 lakh to the families who had lost their sole earning hand.

And to think that the villagers complained how their near and dear ones were lynched in the presence of policemen, among them a deputy superintendent and a circle officer. There will be separate epitaphs for Pehlu Khan and Qasim, Tahir and Rakbar, Noman and Siraj too. Each tombstone will be a tribute to a man who tried to earn his bread and butter through dint of sheer hard work. Each tombstone will be an indictment of the state which failed to protect their lives and a

society that watched on either helplessly or in tacit acceptance. Each one will be accountable to posterity.

Is there a ray of hope? Yes, the Supreme Court's ruling on a series of lynching incidents offers a sliver of hope. It's taking note of an alleged *gau rakshak*'s bragging about killing Qasim and hitting Samiuddin, and that tells us all is not lost. The judiciary is still a well-regarded and respected resort—even Akhlaq's family, after his brutal killing and political support to his killers, expressed hope in the judiciary. And at the social level, if we had Imam Rashidi of Asansol who prevented a communal riot after losing his teenage son Sibghatullah—the boy's body was handed over to the father after his nails had been stabbed out and an eye gouged by rioters—we also have the shining example of the people of Kerala who overcame differences of religion to help each other at the time of the most grave flood for over a century. A mosque in Malappuram gave shelter to 17 Hindu families for days on end. A temple, meanwhile, gave its premises to Muslims to offer their Eid prayers. And a group of Muslim men got busy with cleaning two Hindu temples after the flood had taken its toll. Almost all of them were beefeaters.

VOICE OF SANITY: Imam Rashidi, Who Appealed for Peace despite Losing His Son to Communal Violence in Asansol, Bengal

About the Author

Ziya Us Salam is a noted literary and social commentator.

He has been associated with *The Hindu* for more than 18 years. He has been *The Hindu*'s Features Editor for North India editions for 16 years. At present, he is Associate Editor, *Frontline*, and writes on sociocultural issues for the magazine besides doing book reviews.

His book *Of Saffron Flags and Skullcaps*, published by SAGE, was released in 2018. The same year, *Till Talaq Do Us Part*, a study of various divorce options available in Islam, was released. His book *Delhi 4 Shows*, a study of cinemas since the talkie era began, was released in 2016.

He has contributed to the following anthologies: *Being Young in the Worlds of Islam* and *Past Tense: Living on the Edge*. He has edited an anthology titled *House Full: The Golden Age of Hindi Cinema*.

He was a jury member of the International Film Festival of India (non-feature film, 2011), Best Writing on Cinema (2008) and Vatavaran.

His book *Snapshots of Islam* will be released shortly.

Many serious controversies currently prevalent in our society can be understood in the correct light when we read this book. We will then discover shocking untruths and totally false so-called facts which are accepted today by society, to be the creation of fertile minds intent on dividing Indian society and weakening it.

R. H. Khwaja, IAS (Retd)
Former Secretary to the Government of India

A freedom fighter's account of India's struggle for independence.

For special offers on this and other books from SAGE, write to marketing@sagepub.in

Explore our range at
www.sagepub.in

Paperback
978-93-528-0640-9

This is a book written in anger—anger over the long history of oppression and ruthless exploitation under British rule. It is a scholarly work and is also a powerful political text.

Amar Farooqui
Professor, Department of History, University of Delhi

A freedom fighter's telling account of the exploitation of India by the East India Company.

For special offers on this and other books from SAGE, write to marketing@sagepub.in

Explore our range at
www.sagepub.in

Paperback
978-93-528-0802-1

Extolled for his extraordinary courage, Bhagat Singh is one of our most venerated freedom fighters. He is valourised for his martyrdom, and rightly so, but in the ensuing enthusiasm, most of us forget his contributions as an intellectual and a thinker. In the current political climate, when it has become routine to appropriate Bhagat Singh as a nationalist icon, not much is known about his nationalist vision. This book provides a corrective to this by bringing together a majority of Bhagat Singh's writings, some of which were hitherto unavailable in English.

A collection that brings together Bhagat Singh's seminal writings.

For special offers on this and other books from SAGE, write to marketing@sagepub.in

Explore our range at www.sagepub.in

Paperback
978-93-528-0837-3

Tracing the life of Zarina Bhatty, a Muslim woman born and brought up in pre-Partition India, this memoir narrates the experiences of a woman who strove to break out of the stereotypical roles imposed by the society of her times. It chronicles her life over 80 years, portraying the political and social conditions of undivided and post-Independence India. Zarina's story is a story of grit, perseverance and determination to battle against all odds—a story that was waiting to be told.

An extraordinary Muslim woman's life chronicled.

For special offers on this and other books from SAGE, write to marketing@sagepub.in

Explore our range at www.sagepub.in

Paperback
978-93-528-0665-2